KU-679-207

CONTENTS

GLOBETROTTER™

Travel Guide

ICELAND

ROWLAND MEAD

NEW HOLLAND

NEW
HOLLAND

★★★ Highly recommended
★★ Recommended
★ See if you can

Third edition published in 2005
by New Holland Publishers (UK) Ltd
London • Cape Town • Sydney • Auckland
First published in 2001
10 9 8 7 6 5 4 3 2 1
website: www.newhollandpublishers.com

Garfield House, 86 Edgware Road
London W2 2EA
United Kingdom

80 McKenzie Street
Cape Town 8001
South Africa

14 Aquatic Drive
Frenchs Forest, NSW 2086
Australia

218 Lake Road
Northcote, Auckland
New Zealand

Distributed in the USA by
The Globe Pequot Press, Connecticut

ISBN 1 84537 012 0

Publishing Manager (UK): Simon Pooley
Publishing Manager (SA): Thea Grobbelaar
DTP Cartographic Manager: Genené Hart
Editors: Melany McCallum, Thea Grobbelaar,
Donald Reid
Cartographers: Nicole Bannister, Marlon Christmas
Design and DTP: Éloïse Moss
Picture Researcher: Sonya Meyer
Proofreader: Ingrid Schneider
Consultant: Richard Sale

Reproduction by Hirt & Carter (Pty) Ltd, Cape Town
Printed and bound by Times Offset (M) Sdn. Bhd.,
Malaysia.

Photographic Credits:
J. Arnold/jonarnold.com: cover;
Jenny Forrest: title page, pages 9, 15, 21, 39, 49, 50, 54, 57,
62, 66, 68 (bottom), 80, 81, 82, 83, 85, 86, 87, 92, 95, 96, 97,
102, 106, 107, 112;
Gallo/Tony Stone Images/Paul Chesley: page 22;
Gallo/Tony Stone Images/Jonny Johnson: page 12;
Gallo/Tony Stone Images/Hans Strand: page 7;
Gallo/Tony Stone Images/Kim Westerskov: page 74;
Fiona McLeod: pages 13 (left), 18, 20, 23, 24, 35, 37, 38, 42,
43, 55;
Rowland Mead: pages 14, 25, 48, 53, 64, 65, 72, 76, 77, 78,
79, 94, 98, 100, 105, 108, 109, 110;
Richard Sale: pages 4, 6, 10, 11, 13 (right), 16, 17, 19, 26,
27, 28, 29, 30, 32, 33, 34, 36, 41, 46, 51, 52, 56 (top and bot-
tom), 58, 60, 67, 68 (top), 69, 70, 90, 104, 111, 114, 116, 117,
118, 119, 120.

Keep us Current
Information in travel guides is apt to change, which is
why we regularly update our guides. We'd be grateful
to receive feedback if you've noted something we
should include in our updates. If you have new
information, please share it with us by writing to the
Publishing Manager, Globetrotter, at the office nearest
to you (addresses on this page). The most significant
contribution to each new edition will receive a free
copy of the updated guide.

Cover: *Strokkur geyser erupting.*
Title page: *Turf houses at Skaftafell National Park.*

1
Introducing Iceland

Over the last decade, Iceland has become one of the world's fastest growing tourist destinations. The reasons are easy to appreciate. A volcanically active zone runs through the country from northeast to southwest following a tectonic plate boundary. Active **volcanoes** such as Hekla and Krafla have reared above lava plains and **geothermal areas**, which include geysers, fumeroles, hot springs and mud springs. There are numerous **icecaps**, including Vatnajökull, which is bigger than the rest of Europe's icecaps put together. **Glacier** tongues flow from the icecaps, with icebergs calving from their snouts, sometimes into glacial lagoons, such as that at Jökulsárlón. Steep-sided **fiords**, formed by glaciers, punctuate the northwest and southeast coast, giving shelter for fishing villages. Iceland even has **deserts** – in this case the cold variety. In fact, because of the icecaps, lava fields and deserts, over 70 per cent of the country is uninhabitable.

Iceland has a population of some 290,000, of which two thirds live in the capital, **Reykjavík**, and its suburbs. As well as being one of the least crowded countries in the world, it is also one of the least polluted – all its power is from geothermal sources – and the clear light will delight photographers. The country is a **bird-watchers' joy**, with teeming 'sea-bird cities' on its cliffs and abundant wildfowl on lakes such as Mývatn. Others come to Iceland for **outdoor activities** – hiking, whitewater rafting or snow-mobile rides across an icecap. But do not come here for sun-drenched beaches, as they are composed of black volcanic sand and are pounded by massive Atlantic waves.

TOP ATTRACTIONS

*** **Lake Mývatn:** great range of birds and some fascinating volcanic features.
*** **Geysir Area:** geysers and other geothermal surprises; Gullfoss waterfall and Skáholt Cathedral.
*** **Jökulsárlón:** boat trip on a glacial lagoon amongst melting icebergs.
*** **Hallgrímskirkja:** modern church with superb views over the rooftops of Reykjavík.
*** **Thingvellir:** lakeside site of ancient parliament.
*** **Blue Lagoon:** hot-water swimming pools alongside a geothermal power station.

Opposite: *Thingvellir, the site of Iceland's historical outdoor parliament.*

Above: *A distant view of Vatnajökull, Iceland's largest icecap.*

THE LAND

Situated in the North Atlantic Ocean, just to the south of the Arctic Circle, Iceland covers just over 100,000km² (62,138 sq miles), making it the second largest island in Europe. The nearest land masses are Greenland – 287km (178 miles) to the northwest; Norway – 970km (602 miles) to the east; and Scotland – 798km (495 miles) to the southeast. Iceland is the largest of a series of islands positioned on the submarine mountain chain known as the Mid-Atlantic Ridge, which marks a **plate boundary** separating the American Plate from the Eurasian Plate, which are moving apart at an average rate of 1–2cm (½–1in) a year. Geologists delight in stating that the west of Iceland is in North America and the east of the country is in Europe! It is also true that, geologically speaking, Iceland is the youngest country in Europe.

The **volcanic belt** runs in a northeasterly direction, from the southwest of the country in the Reykanes Peninsula area towards Lake Mývatn. It varies in width from 40km (25 miles) to 60km (40 miles) and is typified by volcanoes and other forms of volcanic activity such as geysers, hot springs, mud springs, fumeroles and solfa-taras. The majority of the lava is of the scoria type, which is coarse, loose and sharp and which often solidifies into fantastic shapes. Volcanic activity has continued through-out recorded history, with the most recent eruptions being at Surtsey in 1963, Heimaey in 1973, Krafla in the mid-70's and Hekla in 1991. In the east and west of Iceland, away from the active volcanic zone, are mountains of basalt and rhyolite, the result of lava flows up to 20 million years ago.

Another important feature in the shaping of Iceland is **ice**. The country is still in the throes of the Ice Age and enormous icecaps can be seen where the land is about 1300m (4265ft) above sea level. The biggest icecap is **Vatnajökull**, the largest in Europe and also the world's third greatest after Antarctica and Greenland. Tongues of ice, called valley **glaciers**, spread out from the icecaps, eroding deep U-shaped valleys and creating a number of spectacular **fiords**. The material eroded by the glaciers is eventually deposited on outwash plains or **sandur** – lowland areas covered with sand, gravel and braided streams. The largest of the sandur is Skeiðarársandur, situated to the south of the Vatnajökull icecap. The juxtaposition of ice and volcanic activity can have calamitous effects, such as the **jökulhlaup**, where volcanic activity under an icecap melts the ice to cause huge amounts of glacial flood water.

> **PLATE TECTONICS**
>
> The modern science of Plate Tectonics has its origins in the work of **Alfred Wegener**, who in 1912 published his work on **Continental Drift**. It was rejected then as he did not suggest a mechanism by which this drift could occur. It is now known that convection currents can move plates in various ways, causing three types of margin: **Constructive Margins**, with plates moving apart and volcanic material forming new land (as in the case of the Mid-Atlantic Ridge in Iceland); **Destructive Margins**, with plates moving together to form fold moun-tains; and **Passive Margins**, where plates move sideways, causing earthquake activity.

Below: *Lingering snow in the Landmannalaugar area on one of the main routes through the interior.*

VOLCANOES

Volcanoes are mountains formed when hot molten lava is forced through weak points in the earth's crust. The material may be liquid, as in the case of **lava**, or solid, as with volcanic **bombs** or **ash**. Steam and gases are also commonly found around volcanoes. Volcanoes generally have a distinct **crater**, which may fill with rain water to form a **crater lake**. The shape of a volcano depends very much on the type of material erupted. The most common volcanic material seen in Iceland is **basalt**, which is a very fluid lava, forming extensive **lava fields**. Those volcanoes which are erupting at present are known as **active**, while those which are totally dead are called **extinct**. Volcanoes which are temporarily quiet are said to be **dormant**.

Mountains and Rivers

Many of Iceland's **rivers** have their sources on the ice-caps, particularly on Vatnajökull. The Skjálfandafljót and the Jökulsá á Fjöllum flow northwards to reach the sea to the west and east of Húsavík, while the Lagarfljót runs northeast through Egilsstaðir on its route to the Atlantic. The main river of the southwest is the Thjórsá, which rises in the interior and arrives at the sea east of Selfoss. The volume of water in Iceland's rivers gives rise to some of the most spectacular **waterfalls** in the world, including Gullfoss, east of Reykjavík, or the magnificent Dettifoss in the northeast. Iceland's highest **mountains** are called **nunataks**, or mountains which rise above the level of the ice. They include Hvannadalshnjúkur, at 2119m (6972ft), and Barðarbunga, at 2009m (6591ft), both on Vatnajökull. Just as spectacular, although not necessarily as high, are Iceland's volcanoes – particularly Hekla, at 1491m (4891ft), which has a perfect cone shape, capped by snow and ice.

Seas and Shores

The hard, volcanic rocks of Iceland have produced some truly majestic **cliffs**, alive with nesting sea birds in the summer. Winds, particularly those from the prevailing southwest, whip up strong waves which erode the cliffs into **sea stacks** and **arches**, such as those at Dyrhólaey, near Vík. In other areas, deep **fiords** provide safe harbours for fishing fleets. Less common are **spits** – these are long ridges of sand and shingle formed by long-shore drift and marine deposition. They are best seen to the east and west of Höfn, where a narrow gap in the spit leads to a sheltered harbour.

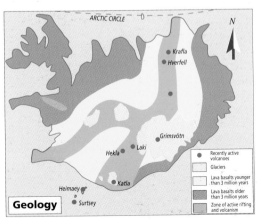

ARCTIC CIRCLE

N

Krafla
Hverfell

Grímsvötn

Hekla   Laki

Heimaey

Katla

Surtsey

Geology

● Recently active volcanoes
☐ Glaciers
☐ Lava basalts younger than 3 million years
▨ Lava basalts older than 3 million years
▨ Zone of active rifting and volcanism

Climate

Iceland's maritime climate is noted in particular for its changeability. The people of Iceland are fond of saying, 'if you don't like the weather right now, just wait a few moments and it will change'. Weather conditions such as wind, rain, snow, hail and fog

COMPARATIVE CLIMATE CHART	REYKJAVÍK				AKUREYRI				EGILSSTAÐIR			
	WIN	SPR	SUM	AUT	WIN	SPR	SUM	AUT	WIN	SPR	SUM	AUT
	JAN	APR	JULY	OCT	JAN	APR	JULY	OCT	JAN	APR	JULY	OCT
AVERAGE TEMP. °C	-0.8	2	11	5	-1.8	3.5	11	3.9	-1.3	1.4	9.9	4.5
AVERAGE TEMP. °F	30.5	35.6	51.8	41	28.7	38.3	51.8	39	29.6	34.5	49.8	40
HOURS OF SUN	1	5	6	2	0.5	5	7	2	1	5	6	2
RAINFALL mm	76	58	52	86	55	29	33	58	134	87	97	169
RAINFALL in	3	2.3	2	3.4	2.1	1.1	1.3	2.3	5.3	3.4	3.8	6.7
DAYS OF RAINFALL	19	17	15	19	16	12	12	17	20	16	15	20

can all feature within a single day, so visitors to this destination need to be prepared for all eventualities.

Iceland's geographical position directly in the path of the **Gulf Stream** combined with the prevailing westerly winds means that winters here are milder than in cities of a more southerly latitude such as Toronto, New York and Moscow. The downside is that though they are less harsh, the winters can be extremely wet, particularly in the southwestern parts of the country around Reykjavík, where the wind makes the climate even more miserable. The situation barely improves in summer, when the capital receives on average only one fine day during the month of July.

Below left: *The Atlantic waves attack the steep cliffs of basalt at Krýsuvíkurberg on the Reykjanes Peninsula.*

TUNDRA AND PERMAFROST

The higher parts of the interior of Iceland have an ecosystem known as the **tundra**. This is a result of the long, severe winters, a short growing season and precipitation which falls mainly as snow. The ground is permanently frozen, apart from the top 50cm (20in) or so which melts in summer. This condition is known as **permafrost**. Because of the permafrost, the surface of the land is often marshy and badly drained in the summer.

Above: *The mighty Gullfoss waterfall is completely frozen in winter.*

LAND OF THE MIDNIGHT SUN

This is a descriptive title which is often applied to Iceland, but it is only partly true. It never really gets dark anywhere in Iceland during June, but to actually be able to see the sun at midnight means going to a location within the Arctic Circle. The only place where this is possible is on the island of Grimsey, about 41km (25 miles) north of Akureyri. Unfortunately for Grimsey, it sees no sun at all during the month of January.

The more eastern and northern fringes of the country, which are in the rain shadow of the central mountains and icecaps, fare rather better from the point of view of sunshine. Akureyri, in the north, is the warmest part of the country and Egilsstaðir, in the east, is the driest. When the wind blows from the Arctic, however, the temperature can drop alarmingly. Fogs are common on the eastern side of the country, particularly when cold ocean currents from the north meet the more temperate Gulf Stream. Snowfall is heavy in the interior of the country, especially on the high icecaps. Much of the interior is only free enough of snow to allow transport during the months of July and August. In the drier cold deserts and sandur, windblown dust and gravel can seriously damage the paintwork of vehicles and make a misery of a cycling holiday. Visitors, however, will also remember Iceland for its clarity of light, largely thanks to the unpolluted environment.

Iceland's position close to the Arctic Circle means that its daylight hours vary considerably between summer and winter. During the winter months of December and January, three to four hours of daylight are as much as can be expected, and Icelanders can suffer from 'short day despression', with suicide rates increasing at this time of the year. One compensation, however, is that this is the best season to see the *aurora borealis*, or Northern Lights. The situation is reversed in the summer, when in June and July daylight continues throughout the night.

Wildlife

One of the main characteristics of the fauna and flora of Iceland is the small number of species to be seen. There are obvious reasons for this – until the end of the Ice Age some 20,000 years ago, Iceland was covered with snow and glaciers. With the climate improving only slowly, the recolonization of plants and animals has been a gradual process, and even today the inhospitable climate and the short growing season are limiting factors. A further reason is the fact that Iceland is an island in an isolated part of the North Atlantic Ocean, making the migration of species difficult.

The only **mammal** which is indigenous to Iceland is the **arctic fox**. Farmers have always blamed the fox for killing lambs, and large numbers have been shot. In fact, the arctic fox lives mainly on small birds and rodents, although it is also a scavenger and can be seen finishing off carcasses of sea birds or sheep. The arctic fox changes the colour of its coat in winter, and a small minority of the species turns completely white. Numbers of arctic foxes have dropped considerably and visitors will be lucky to see this wary animal.

There have been a number of mammals **introduced** inadvertently, particularly rodents. **Reindeer** were brought in from Norway in the 18th century, but as Icelanders did not readily take to the idea of living as nomadic reindeer herders, the animals reverted to the wild. They were often hunted, both for meat and to prevent them grazing valuable sheep pastures, so that their numbers have frequently dropped to dangerously low levels. The reindeer is now a protected species in Iceland,

Below: *The arctic fox, Iceland's only indigenous mammal, is wary of man.*

and they live in scattered groups, mainly in the east of the country. **American mink** were introduced for fur farming in the 1930s, and escaped mink can be found throughout the country in marine and freshwater sites. **Polar bears** from Greenland occasionally reach Iceland on ice flows. As this has been going on throughout history, it seems that polar bears could have established themselves in Iceland, but for the fact that they are usually shot on arrival.

Marine mammals are much more plentiful, with around 20 species regularly visiting Icelandic waters. Both common (or harbour) and grey **seals** breed around the coast, and Iceland has around half the world's total population of common seals – the best time to see them is at the end of June when they are pupping. **Walruses** also occasionally appear, mainly on the northwest coast. Spring and summer are the best times to see **whales**. Since the killing of whales has been banned, a number of Icelandic fishing ports have begun to specialize in whale-watching trips which have proved popular with visitors. The most commonly seen whales are sperm, minke, killer and fin, while common **porpoises** and white-beaked **dolphins** also turn up. Iceland's decision in late 2003 to resume a limited amount of whaling for 'scient-ific purposes' has roused huge international criticism.

There is no doubt that it is the **birds** which comprise the most spectacular part of Iceland's fauna. Although there are only around 70 resident breeding bird species, there are a large number of migrants and accidental visitors, making the Iceland list top well over 300 species. What attracts birders to the country is the rarity of the birds and the fact that they are a curious mixture of European, North American, Arctic and temperate species – three North American

Below: *Since the banning of whaling, orcas or killer whales have become increasingly common in Icelandic waters.*

species, for example (Barrow's goldeneye, the great northern diver and the harlequin duck), are found nowhere else in Europe. Sea birds breed in incredible numbers and include gulls, guillemots, skuas, puffins, razorbills, gannets, kittiwakes, fulmars, shags and cormorants. Iceland has an abundance of wetland sites which provide the ideal breeding habitat for geese, whooper swans and a wide variety of ducks. The most important breeding site is Lake Mývatn, where there are vast numbers of tufted duck, scaup, mallard, pintail, gadwall, wigeon and teal. Wading birds, too, are well represented, though birds of prey are limited to the merlin, the gyrfalcon, the threatened white-tailed sea eagle, and the rare snowy owl.

Iceland's freshwater areas abound with **fish**, but there are only five main varieties: Arctic char, eels, salmon, trout and sticklebacks. Visitors should be aware that licences for salmon fishing are cripplingly expensive. On the other hand, there is a rich variety of **oceanic fish**, including cod, haddock, whiting, plaice, ling, sole, redfish and herring. Of the larger fish, the Greenland shark is common in Iceland, and its meat is a popular delicacy.

Iceland's geographical isolation has meant that certain types of fauna are missing. No butterflies breed, although certain migrants, such as painted ladies, may appear in some years. Iceland has no amphibians, such as frogs, toads and newts. Nor, visitors will be pleased to know, are there any snakes!

Above left: *An eider duck's nest, showing the down that is collected for use in bedding.*
Above right: *The fulmar is Iceland's most common seabird, often nesting on inland cliffs.*

BIRDS YOU WILL NOT SEE

The climate and the natural vegetation of Iceland have a limiting effect on the range of birds to be seen. The lack of mature trees means that many of the **passerine** (perching) birds, such as **warblers**, are missing. So are hole-nesting species such as **woodpeckers**, **nuthatches** and **treecreepers**. The general lack of insect life cuts out **swallows**, **martins** and **swifts**. Furthermore, the often frozen water prohibits **kingfishers**. Nor will you find **penguins** - they are confined to the Antarctic!

Above: *Swathes of Alaskan lupins cover the lower hill slopes in early summer.*

TUNDRA FLORA

Because of the permafrost conditions and the short growing season, plants on the tundra areas of Iceland have barely two months to complete their life-cycles. Such plants must have a very high tolerance to cold and to lack of moisture (water is often unavailable as it is stored as snow or ice). Not surprisingly there are fewer species of plants on the tundra than on any other biome. Plants which do survive tend to be low-growing and rounded in order to gain protection from the wind. Flowering plants can be spectacular, with 'bloom mats' of anemones, arctic poppies, saxifrages and gentians.

Flora

One of the first things that visitors notice about Iceland is the lack of **trees**. For much of the country, dwarf and scrubby willow and birch are the best that can be seen. It is claimed that early inhabitants felled the trees for building materials and fuel, and that sheep prevented regeneration by eating new shoots. Not everyone agrees with this opinion, however, as the Old Norse word for 'woods' is the same as the present-day word for 'willows'. Could it be that the widespread 'forests' were little more than the same scrub seen today? There are two areas of impressive woodland near Hallormsstaðarskógur in the east of the country and at Fnjóskadalur in the north. Many surburban gardens in Reykjavík, helped by a climatic 'heat island', also have a good range of small trees.

The range of **flowering plants** is small but of considerable interest. It is largely of North European character. Early in the summer cushions of moss campion abound, particularly on the mature lava flows. Dandelions and Alaska lupins are also common at this time of the year, while later in the year vast swathes of white cotton grass cover the landscape. On the heathlands and moorlands, low-growing shrubs are dominant and include whortleberry, crowberry and bearberry. Mosses and lichens are found everywhere and are usually the first plants to colonize new lava flows. Geothermal regions develop their own assemblage of heat-loving plants.

HISTORICAL CALENDAR

700s Irish monks live in Iceland.

800s Norse colonization of Iceland begins.

870 The first recognized settler, Ingólfur Arnarson, sets up home in the Reykjavík area.

930 The population reaches around 60,000. Immigrants are mainly people dissatisfied with life in Norway. The Althing – the National Assembly – is set up near Thingvellir Lake.

930–1230 The Saga Age.

990 Leifur Eiríksson discovers North America.

1106 Bishoprics are established at Skálholt and Hólar.

1220 Beginning of the Sturling Period, marked by feuds and violence.

1241 Snorri Sturluson is murdered.

1262 Iceland comes under the Norwegian crown.

1300s Period of disasters, including earthquakes, volcanic eruptions, famines and diseases.

1397 Both Iceland and Norway come under the Danish crown.

1550 Reformation is imposed by the Danish king. The last Catholic bishop is beheaded.

1700s More volcanic activity, including, in 1783, the Laki eruption. Poisonous gases kill over 10,000 people as well as thousands of animals.

1798 The Althing moved from Thingvellir to Reykjavík

1840s Campaign for self-rule led by Jón Sigurðsson.

1904 Home rule is achieved under Danish control.

1940 Denmark is occupied by Germany. The Althing decides that the union with Denmark is now void. Iceland is occupied by British troops as a strategic defence measure.

1941 The USA takes over the defence of Iceland and establishes a base at Keflavík.

1944 Iceland declares an independent republic at Thingvellir on 17 June.

1946 Iceland joins United Nations Organization.

1949 Iceland becomes a founding member of NATO.

1958 The first of the so-called 'Cod Wars' with Britain over fishery rights.

1970 Iceland joins EFTA.

1974 Iceland's 1406km (873-mile) Ring Road is completed.

1980 Vigdís Finnbogadóttir becomes the world's first democratically elected woman President.

1986 Reagan–Gorbachov summit held at Reykjavík.

1990s Tourism begins to develop as a major foreign currency earner.

HISTORY IN BRIEF

Iceland's first recorded inhabitants were Irish monks who came to the area, probably by sea-going coracles, in the 700s. They had fled persecution in their own country and came to Iceland seeking a life of quiet contemplation. These hermits fled when the first Norse settlers came around the year 870. The first known Norseman to reach Icelandic shores was a Viking called Naddodur. He found an unpromising snowy landscape. He called the country 'Snæland' and immediately sailed away. Later, a Swede called Garðar

Below: *Wild flowers are quick to colonize newly weathered soil on glacial moraine and lava flows.*

Opposite: *The 19th-century wooden church at Thingvellir.*
Below: *Statue of Leifur Eiríksson, who is believed to have discovered North America in 990.*

Svavarsson circumnavigated the land, confirming that it was an island. In 860, a third Viking called Flóki Vilgerðson navigated his way to the country with the aid of three ravens. He landed in the Breiðafjörður area, where his party spent the winter. He had neglected, however, to collect enough hay for winter food for his animals, which then perished. He named the island 'Iceland' and returned to Norway.

The settlement of Iceland now gathered pace. The immigrants were mainly from Norway where they were disenchanted with the tyrranical rule of King Harald Fair-hair. It is officially recognized that the first permanent settler was **Ingólfur Arnarson**, who arrived in 874. It is said that Arnarson selected the spot where they put ashore in the traditional Viking way by throwing his high seat pillar overboard and waiting to see where it landed. Arnarson named the area Reykjavík (smoky bay) after the vapours from the local hot springs.

Early Government

The period of settlement was over by 930, when the population had reached asround 25,000. Arnarson's son, Thorsteinn Ingólfsson, founded the first 'thing', or local assembly, and in 930 he was one of the founder members of the **Althing** or general assembly. The assembly was needed because a number of self-ruling groups had sprung up around the country and a code of law became necessary. The site of the Althing was chosen to be on the shores of Lake Thingvellir, where delegates came from all over the country for two weeks every year. New laws were decreed, judgements were passed, criminals were punished and claims settled. The opportunity was also taken for marriages to be arranged and business deals to be concluded. For this purpose, a number of stone

booths were erected and the remains
of these can still be seen today. The
Assembly also elected the influential
law-speaker, whose task was to recite
from memory one third of the country's
laws each year. Around the year 1000,
the Althing decreed that Iceland should
be a **Christian** rather than a pagan
country. Although generally peaceful,
there were times when the Althing
degenerated into chaos as armed
groups took justice into their own
hands and pitched battles resulted.

The Middle Ages

Violence escalated in the mid-13th century, which
became known as the **Sturlung Period**. There were
ferocious power struggles between the more influential
families, the most significant of which were the
descendants of Sturla. A key figure at this time was
Snorri Sturluson, a writer and diplomat. He eventually
fell foul of the Norwegian King Hákon the Old, who
ordered Snorri's death. In the ensuing chaos, Hákon
took over, and by 1262, the Icelanders were forced to
surrender their independence to Norway.

The 14th century was an unhappy time for Icelanders,
with social hardship and a string of natural catastrophes.
Hekla erupted several times and the Black Death reached
Iceland, killing two thirds of the population. In 1380,
both Norway and Iceland came under the rule of
Denmark, following the Kalmar Union. The Danes
imposed the Reformation and Lutheranism on the country
and, when the Catholic Bishop of Hólar resisted the
changes, he and his two sons were summarily beheaded.
In 1602, Denmark introduced a trade monopoly granting
exclusive trading rights in Iceland to Danish and
Swedish firms. The woes of the Icelanders continued into
the 18th century, when a smallpox outbreak killed a
third of the population. There were also frequent natural
disasters, with the eruptions of Hekla and Katla both

THE SAGAS

The age of the Sagas was
from the late 12th to the late
13th centuries. They were
epic stories, written largely
anonymously, about the early
settlers and their struggle to
survive. Human relationships
were described in detail, so
they contain much accurate
historical detail, including the
violent battles and family feuds
of the time. The Sagas were
often recited by a member of
the family while the others
worked. They provided enter-
tainment during the boredom
of the cold winter nights. The
Sagas were written in old
Norse and because of the
isolation of Iceland, the
language has changed little
over the centuries, enabling
Icelanders today to read the
transcribed accounts. Around
40 Sagas were written. The
best known is the *Egils Saga*,
the biography of Egill
Skallagrísson, while the
most popular, because of
the sympathetic characters,
is the *Njáls Saga*.

leading to widespread famine. The most cataclysmic disaster, however, was the eruption, in 1783, of Laki. This went on for 10 months, creating the largest lava field of historical times and producing a poisonous haze which destroyed pasture, crops and 75 per cent of the country's livestock. The resulting famine killed nearly 20 per cent of the population.

Towards Independence

From this low point in Iceland's history, things could only get better, and the 19th century saw the beginnings of the movement towards **independence**. The Althing, which had been abolished by Denmark, was partially restored in Reykjavík. Denmark then lifted the trade restrictions in 1854 and the freedom of the press followed a year later. An important figure at this time was **Jón Sigurðsson**, a scholar and politician, who lobbied for the restoration of free trade and a return to the full powers of the Althing. In 1874, Iceland was given its own constitution and was at last able to handle its own financial matters. In 1918, Denmark recognized Iceland as an independent state, although still within the Kingdom of Denmark, which retained responsibility for defence and foreign affairs. When Germany occupied Denmark in 1940, Iceland took control of its own affairs, requesting complete independence.

World War II was now raging and British troops occupied Iceland, which had no armed forces and would be vulnerable to German attack. In 1941, US forces took over and stayed on after the war, when the main threat came from Russia. On 17 June 1944, Iceland declared itself an **independent republic**. Thousands of Icelanders went to Thingvellir, the site of the original parliament, to celebrate the event.

THE ICELANDIC MANUSCRIPTS

The Sagas and the other historical manuscripts of Iceland were originally written on vellum. When printing was developed in the 16th century, the old parchments lost their significance and many were lost. At the beginning of the 18th century, Árni Magnusson, a lecturer at Copenhagen University, made it his life's work to collect as many Icelandic manuscripts as he could find. Some were destroyed by a fire in Copenhagen in 1728, but those that surviied were bequeathed to the University of Copenhagen. After independence in 1944, the people naturally wanted their manuscripts back. The Danish parliament authorized this in 1965 and the first batch arrived back in Iceland six years later. The complete collection is now housed in the Árni Magnusson Institute, which is part of the University of Reykjavík.

The Modern Era

In the postwar years, Iceland's international participation grew apace when it joined the United Nations, and then in 1949 became one of the founder members of NATO. Iceland also maintained its traditional ties with its Nordic neighbours by becoming part of the Nordic Council.

In 1958 Iceland extended its fishery limits to 20km (12 miles), provoking the first of the **Cod Wars** with Britain. The second Cod War came in 1972, when the limit was extended to 75km (46 miles). The limit was then extended to 320km (200 miles) in 1975, leading to the third Cod War. When Iceland threatened to withdraw from NATO and break off diplomatic relations, Britain was forced to accept the limits. It was Iceland, however, which had to back down over the whaling issue, due to environmental pressure. At the moment the whaling industry in Iceland is dormant.

Iceland made considerable social advances in the postwar years. It was the first country in the world to have a woman president, and had a thriving Women's Party (which amalgamated with smaller parties in order to oppose the Independence Party). It has comprehensive health and education services, clean air and good housing. The unemployment rate is low and life expectancy is high. Today Iceland's living standards are amongst the highest in the world and it is universally recognized as a technologically advanced and stable country.

THE COD WARS

With such a reliance on fish, it was not surprising that Iceland embarked on the so-called 'Cod Wars'. The problem was over-fishing by foreign fleets after the war, particularly British trawlers seeking cod. Iceland responded by increasing its 5km (3-mile) exclusive fishing zone to to 6.5km (4 miles) in 1952 and then successively to 20km (12 miles), 80km (50 miles) and finally 330km (200 miles) in 1975. Each extension sparked confrontations between British gunboats and Icelandic coastguard vessels. However, no lives were lost and a 'truce' was declared in 1975, by which time Britain had established its own 200-mile limit.

Opposite: *Crowds surround the statue of Jón Sigurðsson in Reykjavík on Iceland's National Day.* **Below:** *Iceland's fishing fleet has the benefit of a 330km exclusion zone.*

THE ICELANDIC FLAG

Like other Nordic nations, Iceland's flag is based on the cross: a red cross on a larger white cross, with a blue background. Icelanders say the blue is the sea, the white the icecaps and the red the volcanoes. The intensely patriotic Icelanders brandish flags by the thousand on their National Day in June.

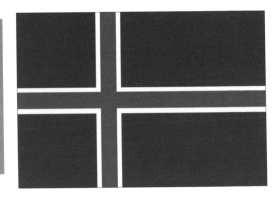

Right: *Icelanders are exceedingly proud of their national flag, which is seen throughout the country, flying from prominent buildings as well as the most humble farmsteads.*
Below: *A man and his toddler celebrate the Icelandic National Day, which is typified by various parades, music and folk dancing.*

GOVERNMENT AND ECONOMY

Iceland has been an independent democratic republic since 1944. The parliament, or Althing, has 63 members elected from eight constituencies for a four-year term. A system of proportional representation is used and every citizen over 18 has the right to vote. The main **political parties** are the right-of-centre Independence Party, which gained 33% of the vote in 2003, and the left-of-centre Alliance Party (31%). Other parties include the Greens, Liberals and the Progressive group. In 2003, 19 of the 63 members elected were woman. The distribution of votes inevitably means that Iceland has a **coalition government**, currently an alliance between the Independence and Progressive parties. Presidential elections also take place on a four-year basis. The current president, elected for a third term in June 2004, is Ólafur Ragnar Grímsson. The president appoints the prime minister, who at the moment is David Oddsson. Relations between them have not always been cordial, particularly since the president recently exercised the power to veto a parliamentary bill for the first time in the Republic's history. Local government is run

on the basis of 23 administrative counties, or *syslur*, subdivided into 200 rural districts, or *hreppur*.

Defence

Iceland has no armed forces of its own apart from a few armed fishery protection and coastguard vessels. Its security is guaranteed by its membership of NATO. The United States has maintained a controversial naval air base at Keflavík since 1951.

Above: *There have been successful experiments in farming salmon, such as in this fiord at Skjálfandi.*

The Economy

Iceland's economy relies heavily on **fishing**, which accounts for over 70% of the country's exports. There are over 900 vessels engaged in fishing, producing an annual catch of around 1.5 million tonnes. The fishing fleet, however, accounts for only 5% of the workforce, with a further 8% involved in fish processing. Fish are exported fresh, frozen, canned and salted. The main fish caught here are cod, redfish, capelin, haddock and saithe. Shellfish include prawns and lobster. Successful experiments have been carried out in salmon and trout farming. The government opposition to joining the EU, is primarily because of Icelanders' fear of losing control over their fishing resources.

Due to the short growing season and the brief, cool summer, only about 1% of the country is devoted to **farming**. Iceland is outside the northern limit of grain production, so the most important crop is hay, which is used as winter food for cattle and sheep. There are over half a million sheep in Iceland and lamb is an important export. In summer, the sheep graze in the highlands so that the better pastures can be used for hay. Farming has become increasingly mechanized and many of the boggy lowlands have been drained. Nevertheless, the number of farm workers has dropped and rural areas have been depopulated as Icelanders increasingly prefer an urban environment. The

---

A FEMALE PRESIDENT

The president in Iceland has a figurehead role, much like that of a monarch in some other countries. In 1980, the Icelanders elected a woman, **Vigdís Finnbogadóttir**, as president. This was the first time that a woman had been democratically elected to the position of president anywhere in the Western World. A popular and respected president, Vigdís was re-elected for three further terms before she stepped down in 1996 to devote herself to other work.

Above: *Geothermal plants supply energy for homes, industry and horticulture.*

remaining farmers have been encouraged to diversify and many make a supplementary living out of tourism by offering farmhouse accommodation. Cheap geothermal electricity has led to the growth of a greenhouse industry, specializing in the production of tomatoes and other salad crops. Flowers and tropical fruits such as bananas are also grown. The industry is centred around Hveragerði in the southwest of Iceland. Many people are employed in the production of both geothermal and hydroelectric energy, the low cost of which has encouraged the development of aluminium smelting and diatom production (*see* page 86).

The largest growth industry is **tourism**. It is currently increasing both its income and the number of tourists who visit the country by 4–5% a year – around 200,000 visitors annually. Accurate statistics are difficult to obtain, however, since many visitors are transit passengers en route to North America or Europe, while others are Icelanders returning from working abroad. Unfortunately, the majority of visitors come to Iceland in the brief summer season from July to August, when there is considerable pressure on accommodation. To overcome this, many boarding schools and colleges are turned into hotels for this period.

Inflation was a problem in Iceland but is currently under control at 2% (2003 estimate). **Unemployment** is low (around 2.8%) and there is even a labour shortage in some areas. Many Icelanders have more than one job in order to maintain a decent standard of living.

THE PEOPLE

It is frequently claimed that Icelanders are, in origin, the 'least Nordic' of the Scandinavian people, with research showing that there is a significant Celtic element in their genes. However, the country does not have a history of absorbing foreigners. Even today, immigration is strictly controlled. Visitors are likely to find that Icelanders are shy upon a first encounter, but this reserve usually gives way to warm hospitality.

Icelandic Names

Most Icelanders have a **patronymic** rather than a family surname, a system which was once common throughout Scandinavia. It is usual for a father, mother, daughter and son each to have a different last name. It works like this: a child takes his father's first name for a surname, to which is added 'son' if the child is a boy or 'dóttir' if a girl. Their own first name is then added. But there are further complications, because a woman retains her own name on marriage. This means that with a family comprising husband, wife, son and daughter, each family member will have a different last name. For example, the father might be called Magnus Jónsson, the son Sigurdur Magnusson, the daughter Gudrún Magnusdottír and the wife Vígdis Kristjándottír. For these reasons, Icelanders always refer to each other by their first name and will expect visiting foreigners to do likewise.

Language

The geographical isolation of Iceland has enabled the country to maintain a language which is similar to Old Norse. The language is closely linked to the culture of the country so that its preservation is a matter of national pride and identity. It has changed so little over time that Icelanders are still able to read the Sagas written over 700 years ago.

COPING WITH THE TELEPHONE DIRECTORY

Hotel guests paging through a telephone directory to ring a business colleague or friend are in for a shock. Firstly, Iceland is such a small place that the whole country can be covered in one directory. Secondly, everyone is listed by their first names, rather than their surnames. This means that there might be three pages of entries under the name of, say, Leifur. Thirdly, a husband and wife living at the same address and sharing a telephone will have separate entries – quite sensible really! Another useful feature is that many Icelanders also list their e-mail address in the directory.

Below: *Icelandic children in traditional woollen hats. In the remote rural areas, children attend boarding school from an early age.*

A LOVE OF BOOKS

Go into any house in Iceland and you will find a well-stocked bookshelf. Icelanders are fiercely proud of their literary tradition, but also, because of their geographical isolation, see books about other parts of the world as a way of broadening their minds. Bookshops abound, not just in Reykjavík, but in many of the smaller settlements. There is a thriving publishing industry in Iceland and it is claimed that more books are published per head of the population than in any other country in the world. Furthermore, one in every ten Icelanders is said to write and publish a book during his or her lifetime.

Below: *A wedding in Akureyri. Many Icelanders, however, will live together rather than marry.*

Sometimes called the 'Latin of the North', Icelandic is a highly complex language and very difficult for non-Nordic people to learn. After mastering their own tongue, Icelanders tend to find other languages easier to learn and many become excellent linguists. They are determined that Icelandic should not be corrupted and and a special academic committee has been formed to find Icelandic words for international terms such as 'computer' and 'mobile phone'.

Iceland has always produced accomplished writers and poets (*skalds*), from the writers of the Sagas and Eddic poems to the present day. In the 19th century, **Jónas Hallgrímsson** was a well-loved romantic poet who was at the forefront of the independence movement and the first Icelander to have a statue raised in his memory. The most important literary figure of the 20th century was undoubtedly **Hálldór Kiljan Laxness**, the winner of the 1955 Nobel Prize for Literature. A one-time monk, communist and film writer, he spent much of his life living abroad, but his novels were largely about the harsh conditions of rural life in Iceland.

Not surprisingly, interest in **books** in Iceland is great. There are over 30 publishers in the country printing over 1000 new titles annually. This is the highest book per capita ratio in the world. There are numerous bookshops, particularly in Reykjavík. In addition, there are five national daily **newspapers**, plus regional papers and countless special-interest magazines. Furthermore there are four TV channels, a national theatre and opera house, many art galleries and numerous museums. Not bad for a population of 278,000!

Religion

The established church in Iceland is the **Evangelical Lutheran Church**, which was made the national church after the Reformation in 1550. Some 96 per cent of the population claim to be Protestants, although only a small fraction attend churches on a regular basis. There are a small number of Roman Catholics, Jehovah's Witnesses and pagan followers of Thor.

Icelanders' attitude towards **marriage** has never been particularly serious. In fact, around 70 per cent of first-born children are born to un-married parents. Single mothers are not frowned upon (a recent president of the country was a single parent), and children are welcomed, whatever the circumstances of their birth.

Above: *This turf church in Núpsstaður is the smallest church in Iceland.*

The Role of Women

Women were given the right to vote in national elections in 1915. They marked the start of the United Nations Women's Decade in 1975 by holding a one-day strike, bringing the whole of Iceland to a standstill. As well as Iceland having a female president, a Women's Alliance political party was also formed and soon gained representation in parliament. This frightened the other political parties so much that they put forward a number of female candidates, which has resulted in the Icelandic parliament having some 22 per cent female MPs. On the employment front, almost 90 per cent of women in Iceland are employed outside the home, but their salaries are still little more than half those of men.

Education

Iceland claims **100 per cent literacy** and certainly education standards are very high. Because of the remoteness of the rural areas of Iceland, many children have to attend boarding school from an early age.

ELVES AND TROLLS

A recent survey found that 53 per cent of Icelanders believed in fairies! Well, let us qualify that – 53 per cent of Icelanders were not pre-pared to deny their existence. In fact, 5 per cent of the population claim to have actually met a fairy, an elf, a troll or one of the 'hidden people'. In a country where the overwhelming majority claim to be Christians, these statistics are perhaps a little surprising. While ghosts were traditionally malevolent beings in Icelandic history, elves tended to be more welcome, and today modern Icelanders are happy to live alongside them – they con-sider the existence of elves to be a 'pleasant idea'.

Those students who go on to complete the secondary grammar stage will be nearly 20 years of age. There are over 5000 students at the University of Iceland in Rekjavík and at its outpost at Akureyri, and usually around 3000 Icelandic students at foreign universities.

Health

Iceland has an excellent National Health service, which is free to all. Icelanders have one of the greatest **life expectancy** figures in the world. Women can expect to live to 80.3 years, men 78.7 – a record which only the Japanese can better. Public health care is no doubt a con-tributing reason for this, but an unpolluted environment and a healthy fish-based diet are also important factors.

Arts and Crafts

Iceland has a long tradition of landscape **painting**, particularly since the beginning of the 20th century. Stalwarts include Ásgrímur Jónsson (1876–1959), Jóhannes Kjarval (1885–1972) and Jón Stefánsson (1881–1962), whose work can be seen in numerous museums and galleries in Reykjavík. Visitors will soon appreciate Iceland's love of **sculpture**, starting at Keflavík airport, the environs of which have some striking modern pieces of work. Statues abound in Reykjavík and other towns, often representing poets and Icelandic heroes rather than politicians and generals. The best-known of the Icelandic sculptors are Ásmundur Sveinsson (1893–1982) and Sigurjón Ólafsson (1908–1982), both of whom have museums devoted to their work in Reykjavík.

Icelandic **craft** work consists mainly of pottery and woollen goods. Many visitors take home woollen jumpers in traditional patterns, which are made from the fleece of the Icelandic sheep. The fleeces contain natural oils which keep out water and the soft inner wool makes a good insulation. The most popular line in ceramics is 'lavaware', which has pieces of lava fired into the clay, but discriminating buyers might consider it to be rather garish.

Food and Drink

Eating out is a major expense for the visitor to Iceland, largely because many food items have to be imported. Icelandic food has traditionally been based on **lamb** and **fish**, which are the most commonly available products. In the past they were preserved for the winter in a variety of ways: smoked, pickled, dried and salted, methods which are reflected in the way in which they are served today. Many of the fish, which include cod, herring, halibut, haddock, salmon and trout, will be familiar to visitors. Other traditional foods include whale steaks, seal, and even sea birds such as puffins. The lack of fresh **vegetables** means that main courses are usually accompanied by such items as potatoes, pickled cabbage and tinned peas or carrots. The growth of the geothermally heated greenhouse industry has served to encourage

---

FRIDAY NIGHT

Iceland appears to foreigners to be a sedate country, so it is something of a surprise for them to find that the nightlife in Reykjavík is amongst the liveliest in Europe. With the high cost of living, youngsters seem to save everything for a huge binge on Friday nights. From 23:00 the whole downtown area of the city is taken over by partying, clubbing young people who move from one venue to the next in what is known as the *rúntur*. Celebrations go on till three or four in the morning. No point trying to sleep – you might as well join in!

Opposite: *Modern sculpture at Keflavík Airport depicting a bird emerging from its egg.*
Below: *Drying fish at Flateyri, northwest Iceland.*

the appearance of various **salads** on many an Icelandic menu in recent years. **Desserts** are usually in the form of cake or dairy produce.

Restaurants in Iceland are generally rather expensive, particularly those in hotels. Fortunately, some offer 'tourist menus' – usually consisting of soup, main course and coffee – at a fixed price, which is normally slightly lower at lunch time. American-style fast-food restaurants are beginning to appear in Reykjavík, but are quite rare outside the capital.

The price of **alcoholic drinks** in Iceland is astro-nomical and visitors are advised to bring their own supplies into the country. Strong beer was prohibited until 1989. Now strong beers from abroad are on sale, and Icelandic beer is also excellent. Wines can be bought with meals but are extremely expensive. The local spirit is *brennivn*, a type of schnapps made from potatoes and flavoured with caraway seed. It is known as 'Black Death' after the name on the label.

Sport and Recreation

Below: *Swimming in hot tubs is a popular social activity throughout Iceland.*

Iceland's most popular recreation is surely **swimming**. Although not great competitors, Icelanders love the social activity of simply lolling around in hot, geo-thermally heated water, even when snow is falling around them. **Football** is very popular and the national team has embarrassed some of the world's top countries in matches in recent years. There are a number of Icelandic professionals who play for clubs overseas, par-ticularly in the English premiership. **Golf** has increased greatly in popularity through the

years, and there are over 20 courses which allow visitors to play. The long winters restrict outdoor activities, so indoor sports are widely played, including **badminton** and **handball**, in which the Icelandic team is one of the best in the world. **Chess** is a national pastime and Iceland boasts no fewer than six grand masters, the highest per capita ratio in the world. **Bridge** is also keenly played, particularly since the national team won the world championship in Japan in 1991. There are **skiing** facilities near many towns in Iceland, although the short hours of daylight in winter are a restricting factor. **Horse riding** was once a necessity for the farming community, though nowadays farming is much more mechanized, and horse riding has become a popular pastime with Icelanders and visitors alike. Freshwater **fishing** is available throughout the country and there are several exclusive salmon fishing clubs. A licence for salmon fishing is extremely expensive, while trout fishing is more reasonably priced. Iceland has become one of the prime venues for **outdoor adventure activities**. Among the activities on offer are hiking and trekking, mountain biking, mountaineering and river rafting. Icelanders also have a fascination with cross-country touring on snowmobiles and in super jeeps.

Above: *Upskiing is one of the more unusual types of recreation in Iceland.*

THE GOLFING PHENOMENON

Considering Iceland's inhospitable climate and lack of daylight for much of the year, it is perhaps surprising that golf has become so popular. There are believed to be 40 courses in Iceland, ranging from 5-hole tracts built by enthusiastic local farmers to 18-hole international standard courses on the outskirts of Reykjavík. Visitors are welcome at the 28 golf clubs in Iceland, but be prepared for some high green fees. The most novel competition is the Arctic Open at Akureyri, which takes place in midsummer, allowing players to tee off at midnight and play through the night.

2
Reykjavík

When **Ingólfur Arnarson**, Iceland's first recognized settler, threw his high seat pillars overboard, they washed ashore at a small peninsula in southwest Iceland. In the Viking tradition, he decided that this would be the place where he would settle. The year was 874. He called the place Reykjavík, which loosely translates as 'smoky bay', on account of the steam rising from the hot springs in the area. Today, 'smokeless bay' would be a more apt description, as Iceland's capital is one of the least polluted cities in the world. Despite this early settlement, Reykjavík was slow to grow. Two factors, however, accelerated the process. Firstly, in the mid-1700s, a businessman named **Skúli Magnusson** set up a number of local industries in an attempt to break the Danish trade barriers. His small factories attracted workers from the surrounding rural area. Secondly, the **Althing** was relocated, moving from Thingvellir to Reykjavík. Nevertheless, at the beginning of the 19th century, there were still only 300 inhabitants in the town. By the end of the century the population had grown to 2000. The steady growth continued and by Independence Day in 1944 the number of inhabitants stood at 45,000. Today that figure has nearly quadrupled at 170,000 and over half of Iceland's population now lives in the capital city.

Reykjavík is the world's most northerly capital and despite its small size it has a university, a National Theatre, a symphony orchestra and an opera house, plus all the other features one would expect to find in a capital city. Visitors to Reykjavík will find that Icelanders

DON'T MISS

*** The Hallgrímskirkja: a modernistic church with great views from its tower over the city and harbour.
*** Tjörnin: city-centre lake full of wildfowl; City Hall stands in northwest corner.
** Öskjuhlíð: a hilltop crowned by the city's water tanks and a revolving restaurant.
** Bernhöftstorfan: a group of old wooden buildings at the western end of Bankastræti.
** Austurvöllur: a pleasant city square, near parliament and the Lutheran Cathedral.

Opposite: *The distinctive Hallgrímskirkja, Reykjavík's most famous landmark.*

Opposite: *Eider ducks are among the many wildfowl found on Tjörnin lake.*
Below: *A variety of buildings and architectural styles on the harbourside.*

are proud of their landscape and, both in the rural areas and in the city, litter, thankfully, is not tolerated. Street crime, too, is minimal and there is probably no safer city in the world than Reykjavík.

THE OLD TOWN

The old town, where most of the important buildings in Reykjavík are to be found, is a compact area which can easily be covered on foot. The most readily recognizable feature is the **Tjörnin**, or pond – a small lake which is a haven for wildfowl. Built partly over the lake is the new Town Hall, or **Rádhús**. Just to the north is the pleasant square known as the **Austurvöllur**, where Ingólfur Arnarson originally had his hayfields. At the side of the square is the **Althingshúsið**, or parliament house, and away to the east are the main shopping streets. Few visitors will want to miss seeing the modern church called the **Hallgrímskirkja**. From the top of its tower a panoramic view stretches across the city's rooftops. Another good view can be had from the **Perlan** (the Pearl), a restaurant perched on top of the city's hot-water storage tanks. Add the many museums and art galleries and there is plenty to occupy the visitor for several days.

Around the Tjörnin ★★★

In the heart of the old town is the **Tourist Information Centre (TIC)**, located in the middle of a group of wooden buildings at Bankastræti 2. The whole complex, known as **Bernhöftstorfan** (or Bernhoft's group) was saved from redevelopment a few years ago. A city map is available, along with a host of brochures, videos and maps of Iceland. The helpful staff can arrange accommodation and book tours. Particularly useful to visitors are the English-language publications *Around Iceland*, *Around Reykjavík*, *What's on in Reykjavík* and *Iceland Explorer*. The TIC is open daily 08:30–18:00 in summer, and 10:00–16:00 during the winter. It is closed on Sundays.

From the TIC take the short walk to the **Tjörnin**. Warm springs keep this lake ice-free in winter so it is an all-year-round haven for birds. Identification boards help visitors to name the wildfowl, including the handsome eider ducks, which are found throughout Iceland. Arctic terns, which spend the winter in the Antarctic, breed on rafts in the centre of the lake, and whooper swans can usually be seen in the summer. Over 40 species of birds have been recorded at this lake. In the northwestern corner of the Tjörnin is the **Rádhús**, or Town Hall. It is ultramodern in

EIDER DUCKS

One of the first birds the visitor to Iceland will see is the eider duck, which breeds on the **Tjörnin Lake** in the centre of Reykjavík. The drake is handsome, with black, white and green plumage, while the female is a drab brown. They are essentially **marine ducks**, but will breed on lakes and rivers close to the coast. The female lines the nest with down from her own breast. The **down** has been used for centuries for stuffing pillows. The **eggs** are also eaten, and the eider duck has been semi-domesticated in Iceland. After hatching, the eider ducklings gather together in a crèche, often consisting of over 30 birds, looked after by one or two of the females.

Above: *Reykjavík's modern Rádhús, or town hall, is built into the waters of Lake Tjörnin right in the centre of the city.*

WALKING IN REYKJAVÍK

Many of the sights of compact central Reykjavík can be reached on foot, but the visitor can also access other areas within the city limits by following set **walking trails**. These walks cover the sea shore, heaths and valleys, and usually link up with bus routes. You can expect to be accompanied by joggers and mountain bikers. For further information on Reykjavík's walking trails, contact the **Tourist Information Centre**, Bankastræti 2, tel: 562 3045.

---

design and built partially on stilts over the lake. Completed in 1992, its design was controversial, because many people felt that it was out of place in the old part of the city. The entrance hall is well worth a look – there is an information desk and a huge relief map of Iceland. Away to the southwest of the lake are the modern buildings comprising the **University of Iceland**, which was established in 1911 and now has over 5000 students. Amongst the university buildings is the **Árni Magnússon Institute**, which was named after the man who, in the 18th century, did much to track down the original manuscripts of the Sagas and Eddas. The institute is open daily in summer from 13:00–17:00, with reduced hours in winter. Also on the university site is the **Nordic House**, which acts as a cultural link between Iceland and the other Nordic countries. Documentary films are shown daily and there are information evenings for tourists. The Nordic House is open from 09:00–16:30 and has an excellent cafeteria.

Austurvöllur ***

Just to the north of the Tjörnin is the attractive square known as the **Austurvöllur**, occupying land which was once Ingólfur Arnarson's farm. In the centre of the square is a **Statue of Jón Sigurðsson** (1811-1879), who led the 19th-century independence movement in Iceland. Built on the southern side of the Austurvöllur is the **Althingishúsið**, or Parliament House. This dull, grey basalt building was constructed in 1881, before Iceland's independence from Denmark, which explains the Danish coat of arms on the front of the building. On the south-eastern side of the Austurvöllur is the **Dómkirkjan**, or Lutheran Cathedral. It dates from 1796, when it was built on the orders of the Danish King. The inside is more interesting than the rather ordinary exterior. Look out for the modern font, made by the Danish sculptor Berthel Thorvaldsen. The Dómkirkjan is open on week-days (except Wednesdays) from 10:00–17:00.

Around Arnarhóll ★★★

Located along Lækjargata is the **Stjórnarráðið**, or Government House. Built between 1765 and 1770, this whitewashed building was once a prison, but now con-tains the offices of the prime minister. A short distance to the north of Government House is a low, grassy hillock known as **Arnarhóll** (Eagle Hill). On the summit is a statue of Ingólfur Arnarson, Iceland's first official settler, shown looking out of his boat towards the land he was to make his home. The most interesting, and oldest, street in the area is **Aðalstræti**, which was where Skúli Magnusson set up his cottage industries in the mid-18th century. The oldest house is number 10, which dates back to 1752. It was once a small weaving workshop, but is now a popular restaurant.

Below: *Icelandic children proudly wear traditional costumes on National Day.*

Rooftop Views ***

There are two popular places to go for good views over the city: the Hallgrímskirkja and the Öskjuhlíð. **Hallgrímskirkja**, just to the east of the city centre, is often mistaken for the cathedral. Completed in 1974, it was built in memory of the Reverend Hallgrímur Pétursson, a noted composer of hymns. The church has one of the geological designs for which Iceland is noted, with its white-coloured west end built of basalt-like columns, which soar up to a graceful tower, some 75m (246ft) in height. The style of the austere interior is traditional Gothic, but most visitors come to take the lift to the top of the tower accompanied by taped choral music, for the superb view over Reykjavík. The church and tower are open from 10:00–18:00. On the green in front of the Hallgrímskirkja is a statue of Leifur Eiríksson, a gift from the USA to celebrate the 1000th anniversary of the Althing.

Öskjuhlíð, a hill which overlooks the domestic airport and the bay, is another good viewpoint. The summit has some old bunkers and gun emplacements, relics of World War II. Also perched on top of the hill is a group of hot-water storage tanks which supply the rather sulphur-smelling hot water to the city. A revolving restaurant called the **Perlan** (Pearl) is on top of the tanks. Also here is the Saga Museum (*see* page 39).

Below: *The clarity of this panoramic view – from the top of the Hallgrímskirkja tower over Reykjavík – is due to the lack of pollution.*

THE HARBOUR

Reykjavík's harbourside is full of interest. The shoreline here was once marked by **Hafnarstræti** (Harbour Street), but the waterfront was extended during World War II. The Customs House, on Hafnarstræti, has some excellent 19th-century houses on its southern side. The harbourside is the regular venue for the **Kolaportið flea market**, where some great bargains can be found, particularly home-made woollen goods. At the eastern end of the harbour, off Sæbraut, is probably the most remarkable of all the many sculptures in the city; the **Viking Ship**, by Jón Gunnar Árnason, is very photogenic.

Above: *Of all the artworks in Reykjavík, this harbourside sculpture of a Viking boat, the work of Jón Gunnar Árnason, is the most distinctive.*

MUSEUMS AND GALLERIES

The National Museum *

Founded in 1863, the National Museum moved to its present location on Hringbraut (entrance in Suðurgata) in 1950. It has over 16,000 artefacts from Viking times to the present, including costumes, agricultural implements, nautical equipment, furniture and boats. The most famous item is the wooden church door from Valpjófsstaður. This door was carved in the 13th century and depicts a Norse battle scene. The museum is open 10:00–18:00 in summer and 11:00–17:00 in winter; closed on Mondays.

Listasafn Íslands (National Gallery of Iceland) *

Located just behind the Fríkirkjan (or Free Church) at Fríkirkjuvegur 7, this building has a chequered history. Originally a storage space for ice cut from Lake Tjörnin, it later became a nightclub, before a fire reduced it to a shell in 1971. It was then renovated to house the picture collection from the National Museum. There are also some visiting exhibitions. Open 12:00–18:00, Tuesday–Sunday. Admission is free, except for special exhibitions.

IN PURSUIT OF SALMON

Reykjavík is unique as a capital city in having a first-class salmon river running within its boundaries. But visitors beware! Any salmon caught in Iceland is likely to be one of the most pricey caught anywhere in the world! A licence to catch salmon is extremely **expensive**. Add the price of a guide, equipment and transportation and you have some of the most costly angling imaginable. Fortunately there is the cheaper option of fishing for char and trout. Contact the **Angling Club of Reykjavík**, tel: 568 6050.

Above: *The city's hot water storage tanks are the unusual location for the Pearl Restaurant.*

A MAN-MADE GEYSER

Visitors to the revolving **Pearl Restaurant** on Öskjuhlíð hill are now treated to an additional attraction besides the view. An automatic geyser has been installed. It is not mechanical, but designed on the same principle which causes natural geysers to spout. Superheated geothermal water enters a tapering tube under pressure. Eventually the pressure builds up to such an extent that an eruption of water occurs every five minutes or so. The pipe then refills and the cycle is repeated.

Ásmundur Sveinsson Museum ★

Located on Sigtun, in the east of the city, this museum is in a remarkable igloo-shaped building, designed by the sculptor himself. Although he spent a great part of his life abroad, the themes of Sveinsson's work come from Icelandic folklore. The museum's garden is full of the sculptor's abstract concrete figures. Open in summer from 10:00–16:00, in winter from 13:00–16:00. Ásmundur Sveinsson's house is at Freyjugata 41, opposite the Hallgrímskirkja, and also houses the Iceland Labour Union's Art Gallery. Open daily from 14:00–19:00.

Einar Jónsson Museum ★

This cube-shaped building, designed by the sculptor, is also near the Hallgrímskirkja. The most mystic of all the Icelandic sculptors, Jónsson's only traditional work is the statue of Jón Sigurðsson in the Austurvöllur. Open June–September, 13:30–16:00, but closed on Mondays.

Kjarvalsstaðir ★

Located in Miklatún Park, the Kjarvalsstaðir (Municipal Art Gallery) displays the works of Iceland's best-known artist, the surrealist painter Jóhannes Kjarval (1885–1972). His work is displayed in two large rooms, but there are also numerous exhibitions by other painters, both Icelandic and international. Open 10:00–18:00 daily.

Numismatic Museum *

This museum, at Einholt 4, near the Kjarvalsstaðir, houses collection of coins, medals, military decorations and related books. Open weekdays only, from 09:00–17:00.

Natural History Museum *

Situated at Hverfisgata 116, near Hlemmur bus station, this museum has a large collection of rocks, minerals and indigenous flora and fauna. Open Tuesday, Thursday, Saturday and Sunday, 13:30–16:00. Admission fee.

Sigurjón Ólafsson Museum *

This museum, located at Laugarnestangi 70, between Laugardalur and the harbour, displays a collection of this sculptor's work. Opening times of the museum vary.

Museum of Photography *

A collection of ancient and modern photographs as well as photographic equipment, at Borgartún 1. Open weekdays from 12:00–15:30.

Saga Museum *

Realistic dioramas of important moments in Iceland's history; in the Perlan complex and hot water tanks on Öskjuhlíð hill. Open 10:00–18:00 Jun–Aug.

Árbæjarsafn (Open Air Museum) *

Based on a mid-15th-century farm on the eastern outskirts of the city, Árbæjarsafn is a collection of ancient farm buildings and homes from around the

Below: *The Natural History Museum has a fine collection of geological specimens.*

THE MANIA FOR SWIMMING

Swimming is undoubtedly the most common pastime in Iceland. Swimming lessons are compulsory in schools and no student can graduate from secondary school without passing a swimming test. Reykjavík has no fewer than **nine swimming pools**, all open air, thanks to to the country's geothermal water, which is a compensation for the cool climate. Icelanders like nothing better than soaking in a hot pool with snow falling on them! Visitors using the pools should remember that a **high standard of hygiene** is expected. It is compulsory to wash and soap thoroughly (including the hair), without a swimsuit on, before entering a pool. Enjoy the **hot pots** around the pool. These are a type of jacuzzi, with temperatures kept at around 44°C (108°F).

country, and re-assembled on the site. They include a turf church (1842) from the Skagafjörður area, numerous barns and a sheep hut. There are also transport items, including the only locomotive to run in Iceland (used to construct Reykjavík harbour). Open in summer only, daily except Monday, 10:00–18:00. Admission fee.

The Icelandic Phallological Museum

This museum contains a variety of phallic specimens belonging to the mammals of Iceland. Open 14:00–17:00 Tue and Sat, Sep–Apr; Tue–Sat, May–Aug; tel: 566 8668, 561 6663 or 552 6466, or e-mail: phallus@ismennt.is

OTHER PLACES OF INTEREST
Höfði House *

This building, in Borgartún, close to the shore, is used for civic receptions and functions. Its main claim to fame is that it was the venue for the Reagan–Gorbachev summit in 1986. There is a superb sculpture in the front of the building by Sigurjón Ólafsson.

Botanical Gardens *

Some 65 per cent of Iceland's plants are found in these gardens in the Laugardalur area in the east of the city.

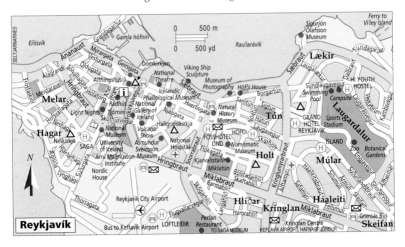

The collection was started by a local citizen and bought by the city authorities in 1955. Open on weekdays in summer from 08:00–22:00, and weekends from 10:00–22:00. During Winter they are open from sunrise to sunset .

Laugadalur *

This open space located in the east of the city, is the main sport and recreation area. It has Reykjavík's largest open-air geothermally heated swimming pool, a football stadium, ski slopes, the Botanical Gardens, a zoo, and an ice-skating rink.

Above: *Children enjoy a puppet show on the shores of Lake Tjörnin.*

Ellidaár River *

Reykjavík is probably the only capital city in the world with a salmon fishing river within its boundaries. The Ellidaár River is in the eastern suburbs and is fed from Lake Ellidaár (which is excellent for trout fishing). The best time to watch the salmon leaping their way up-stream is during late July and early August.

ENTERTAINMENT IN REYKJAVÍK

Reykjavík's **National Theatre** is located at Hverfisgata 19. It does perform operas and ballets, but concentrates mainly on plays. The building itself is of interest, with the interior said to be inspired by the basaltic columns of the Svartifoss waterfall in Southern Iceland. Reykjavík also has a **Symphony Orchestra** and an **Opera Company**; the main tourist office will have details of performances. There are seven **cinemas** in the city. Films are screened in their original language and have Icelandic subtitles. There are two **shows** which will appeal to tourists. The **Volcano Show** is based in a small film theatre at Hellusund 6a near Tjörnin Lake. The films are the work of two Icelandic photographers who have recorded all

> **WHERE ARE ALL THE CATS AND DOGS?**
>
> It slowly dawns on visitors that Icelanders keep few pets. Cats are rarely seen and any dogs noticed are likely to be working animals on farms. In fact, the Iceland government decided that it was unhygenic to keep dogs in city apartments and for years they were banned in Reykjavík. The law has recently been repealed, but dogs are still rare in the city.

the eruptions in the country for the last 40 years, and include the award-winning *Birth of an Island*, describing the growth of Surtsey in the Westmann Islands. The Volcano Show is essential viewing for all visitors going on to the volcanic parts of the country. There are three performances a day in English, and also programmes in French and German.

Light Nights, which is shown at Tjarnargata 10e, is performed in English and is an interesting account of the settlement of Iceland and of the Sagas. Performances, which last about two hours, run nightly (except on Sundays) during the summer. There are a vast number of **pubs** and **discos** in Reykjavík, but none are cheap. They are crowded at weekends, but rarely start to liven up until around 23:00.

GREATER REYKJAVÍK

Stretching away from the city centre are very pleasant suburbs of detached houses and low-rise apartment blocks. As more and more Icelanders move from the rural areas to the capital city, the suburbs of Reykjavík advance across the lava plains. The skill of Iceland's architects ensures that even the apartments have a certain flair and the design is never dull. Gardens are attractive and there are probably more mature trees in Reykjavík than in the rest of the island. Amongst the suburbs is the occasional shopping mall, such as the modern **Kringlan Centre** in the east of the city. Further out is Greater Reykjavík, with its rather characterless settlements. An exception is **Hafnarfjörður**, which is an interesting town in its own right.

DOMESTIC ARCHITECTURE

Builders in Iceland have always had a shortage of timber. Even driftwood found on the beach was a valuable commodity. Wealthy people could import wood from Norway. Stone was impractical for building as volcanic rock, particularly lava, can rarely be cut to suitable shapes. For the ordinary person turf was the common building material, so it is not surprising that few buildings have survived from before the 18th century. During the 20th century, materials such as concrete and corrugated iron became available and these are dominant today. Most Icelanders live in detached houses, but in Reykjavík there are some low-rise apartment blocks of imaginative design.

Located at the end of the Reykjavík Peninsula is the pleasant suburb of **Seltjarnes**, from where there are often good views across the sea northwards to the icecap of Snæfellsjökull. The National Medical Museum, or Nesstofa, is housed in an 18th-century stone building in Seltjarnes. It is open daily in summer from 13:00–17:00. Immediately to the south of the city is the suburb of **Kópavogur**. Its main claim to fame is that, with 20,000 residents, it is Iceland's second largest community. Further south is **Garðabær**, which is considered to be Reykjavík's most elite suburb. Away to the southwest is **Hafnarfjörður** which, although part of Greater Reykjavík, is a town in its own right and is therefore described in Chapter 3, which deals with the Reykjanes Peninsula. East of Reykjavík, and immediately outside its boundary, is the fast-growing town of **Mosfellsbær**, with a population approaching 5000.

A very popular excursion from Reykjavík is a trip to **Viðey Island**, located a few kilometres north of the mainland. During summer, ferries run hourly from Sundahöfn harbour to Viðey. The island, which is situated on an extinct volcano, has been a religious centre since the 12th century and the second oldest church in Iceland is found here. There are some pleasant walks and fine basalt cliffs to see.

Opposite: *Traditional wooden houses in the inner suburbs of Reykjavík, with the spire of the Hallgríms-kirkja in the distance.*
Left: *A lift takes visitors to the top of Hallgrímskirkja, from which there are stunning views over the city and the harbour.*

44

Reykjavík at a Glance

BEST TIMES TO VISIT

Because of the climate and relative hours of daylight and darkness, most tourists visit Reykjavík during the summer peak season of June–August. The tourist authorities want to extend the season into spring and autumn with 'city breaks' to Reykjavík, where the lively nightlife attracts visitors at times such as New Year.

GETTING THERE

The majority of visitors arrive by plane via Keflavík airport, some 48km (30 miles) from Reykjavík. Buses meet every incoming flight, departing 45 minutes after arrival and taking travellers to Icelandair's terminal, which is at the Hotel Lofteiðir. Visitors using the car ferry will arrive at Seyðisfjörður on the east coast and have a long car or coach journey of around 740km (460 miles) to Reykjavík using the Ring Road.

GETTING AROUND

Reykjavík's **taxis** are cheaper than one might expect and tipping is not required. **Bicycles** can be hired economically, but the constant wind in Reykjavík makes cycling difficult. **Buses** offer cheap and convenient transport and the two main terminals are at Lækjartorg and Hlemmur (which has a tourist information desk). A free map of the bus routes is provided by the TIC. There is a standard fare for all routes and distances.

Drivers do not give change. The **Reykjavík Tourist Card** (obtained from the City Hall) provides unlimited use of the city's buses and free admission to some museums and swimming pools. A useful service is the **museum bus** which runs during summer and connects the city's main museums.

WHERE TO STAY

Accommodation in Reykjavík ranges from luxury international **hotels** to **guesthouses** and **hostels**. A significant number close during winter. **Camp sites** are only open in summer.

LUXURY

Grand Hotel Reykjavík, Sigtún 38–105, Reykjavík, tel: 514 8000, fax: 514 8030. Business hotel in a quiet location near Kringlan Centre.
Hotel Loftleiðir, v/Hlíðarfót 101 Reykjavík, tel: 505 0900, fax: 505 0905, e-mail: icehotel@icehotel.is Pool, sauna, restaurants.
Hotel Saga, Hagatorg 1, 107 Reykjavík, tel: 525 9900, fax: 525 9909, e-mail: hotelsaga@hotelsaga.is Modern building, 330 rooms, pool, sauna, restaurant, shops. Sveinsson sculpture outside.

MID-RANGE

Guesthouse Aurora, Freyjugata 24, 101 Reykjavík, tel: 552 5515, fax: 551 4894, e-mail: aurora@simi.is Attractive traditional house in downtown Reykjavík.

Guesthouse Guðmundur Jónasson, Borgartún 34, tel: 511 1500, fax: 515 1511. East of city centre, widely used by guests of Jónasson Tours.
Hotel Borg, Pósthússtræti 11, tel: 551 1440, fax: 551 1420. A 30s-style building with a central location.
Hotel Skjaldbreið, Langavegur 16, 101 Reykjavík, tel: 511 6060, fax: 511 6070. Well-equipped rooms on main shopping street.

BUDGET

Guesthouse Baldursbrá, Laufásvegur 4, 101 Reykjavík, tel: 552 6646, fax: 562 6647. Simple, basic rooms and shared bathrooms and hot tub.
HI Youth Hostel, Sundlaugavegur 34, tel: 553 8110, fax: 588 9201. Next to campsite in Laugardalur. Closed 20 December to 5 January. Advance booking essential in summer.
Salvation Army Guesthouse, Kirkjustræti 2, tel: 561 3203, fax: 561 3315. Simple rooms in the heart of the city.

CAMPING

The campsite at **Laugardalur** and is open 15 May to 15 Sep. It can be crowded in July and August. Showers, laundry and cooking facilities. Daily morning Flybus to Keflavík Airport.

WHERE TO EAT

There is a range of restaurants in central Reykjavík and the suburbs. Though food is a big expense for visitors, bargains

Reykjavík at a Glance

can be found, particularly with lunchtime tourist menus.

LUXURY

Perlan (The Pearl), Öskjuhlið hill, tel: 562 0200. Spectacularly sited on top of city's water tanks; revolves to give views over Reykjavík. Very expensive.
Lækjarbrekka, Bankastræti 2, tel: 551 4430. Gourmet seafood and lamb in a traditional wooden building near TIC.
Jónotan Livingston Mávur, Tryggvagata 3–6, tel: 551 5520. Seafood restaurant near harbour, with aquarium.

MID-RANGE

Á Næstu Grösum (One Woman Restaurant), Laugavegur 20b, tel: 552 8410. Vegetarian, health food; organic wine.
Asia, Laugavegur 10, tel: 562 6210. Oriental cooking.
Fógetinn, Aðalstræti 10, tel: 551 6323. Reykjavík's oldest house; Skúli Magnusson had a weaving shed here. Traditional Icelandic food; live music.
Naust, Vesturgata 6-8, close to the harbour, tel: 551 7759. Offers a range of seafood.

BUDGET

Fast-food outlets include **Pizza Hut** at the Hotel Esja, **McDonalds**, at Austurstræti and Suðurlandsbraut, **Kentucky Fried Chicken** at Faxafen 2, and **Hard Rock Café** at the Kringlan Centre. **Kaffi**, Austurstræti, Reykjavík, tel: 552 2615. Student-style café, good value, hearty meals.

SHOPPING

Reykjavík's main downtown shopping streets are Bankastræti, Laugavegur, and Austurstræti. Skólavoðustígur, which connects Laugavegur with the Hallgrímskirkja, has chic boutiques and craft shops. Many larger shops have moved from the city centre to the new **Kringlan Mall**, which has over 100 shops, plus cinemas, pubs, restaurants and banks, making it an 'alternative city centre', particularly attractive in winter. Despite its reputation as an expensive city, you can find bargains in woollen goods at the Handknitting Association of Iceland (Skólavöðustígur 19) and the Icelandic Crafts Centre (at Hafnarstræti 3). Homemade woollen goods can be bought cheaply at the Kolaportið Flea Market near the harbour. For various crafts, visit the Icelandic Craft House at Lækjargata 4, close to the Tourist Information Centre. There are a number of fine bookshops, including Mál og Menning (at Laugavegur 18) and Eymundsson (in Austurstræti). Last-minute shopping at Keflavík Airport's duty-free shop includes Iclandic products such as vacuum-packed fish.

TOURS AND EXCURSIONS

A popular excursion for visitors to Reykjavík is a relaxing trip to the **Blue Lagoon** in the Reykanes Peninsula, usually combined with a visit to the Hafnir aquarium or local bird cliffs. More demanding is the **Golden Circle Tour**, stopping at the greenhouse town of Hveragerði, the volcanic crater of Kerið, Skálholt Cathedral, Gullfoss, Geysir and Thingvellir – more than enough for a day. Most travel agencies also offer a **City Tour of Reykjavík**.

USEFUL CONTACTS

Tourist Information Centre, Bankastræti 2, tel: 562 3045, fax: 562 4749.
Iceland Tourist Bureau, Skógarhlíð 18, tel: 562 3300.
BSÍ Travel, Umferðarmið-stödin, Vatnsmyraveg 10. A consortium of bus operators, tours throughout the country.
Farm Holidays, Hotel Saga, Reykjavík, tel: 568 3640.
Reykjavik Excursions, Bankastræti 2, tel: 562 4422, fax: 562 4450. Widely used agency for day trips from the capital.
Guðmundar Jónasson Travel, Borgartún 34, tel: 511 1515, fax: 511 1511. Organizes coach and camping tours.

REYKJAVÍK	J	F	M	A	M	J	J	A	S	O	N	D
AVE. TEMP. °C	-0.4	-1.6	-1.5	0.4	7.2	9.8	11.6	11.1	6.6	5.0	3.7	-0.3
AVE. TEMP. °F	30.9	29.9	30.4	37.7	44.9	49.6	52.8	51.9	43.8	41.0	38.6	31.4
AVE. RAINFALL mm	75.6	71.8	81.8	58.3	43.8	50	51.8	61.8	66.5	85.6	72.5	78.7
AVE. RAINFALL in	2.97	2.83	3.22	2.29	1.73	1.97	2.04	2.43	2.62	3.37	2.86	3.1

3
Around Reykjavík

The area to the east and south of Reykjavík is the only part of Iceland which some short-term visitors see. Fortunately it boasts many of the essential historical and geological features which make the country so fascinating. The **Mid-Atlantic Ridge** runs through the area from northeast to southwest. Frequent volcanic eruptions over recent geological time have left extensive lava flows on the Reykjanes Peninsula – a desolate scene for travellers arriving at Keflavík Airport. Further inland, there are volcanoes such as **Hekla** and explosion craters such as **Kerið**, but the star attractions are the geothermal features in the **Geysir** region – where the geyser **Strokkur** performs reliably every three minutes or so – along with the amazing **Gullfoss** waterfall.

The area to the east of Reykjavík is one of the most fertile in Iceland and the two main market towns are **Selfoss** and **Hveragerði**. At the latter, the local geothermal heat is harnessed for electricity, which is the basis for a significant greenhouse agriculture, while the lovely lakeside resort of **Laugarvatn** is popular with weekenders from Reykjavík.

This part of Iceland is steeped in history. Most tours visit the religious centre of **Skálholt**, with its small modern cathedral. Away to the northwest is Iceland's largest lake – **Thingvallavatn**. At its northern end is the **Thingvellir** historical area, which was the site of the annual Althing, an outdoor parliamentary assembly, which first functioned in 930 and witnessed the birth of the modern Icelandic Republic in 1944.

DON'T MISS

*** **Gullfoss:** Iceland's most visited waterfall.
*** **The Great Geysir Area:** fumeroles, mud springs, hot springs and Strokkur geyser.
*** **Thingvellir Historical Site:** location of Iceland's ancient outdoor parliament
*** **The Blue Lagoon:** bathe in the healthy, warm lake, surrounded by lava flows.
* **Krýsuvíkurberg and Hafnaberg:** sea-bird cliffs on the Reykjanes Peninsula.
* **Kerið:** explosion crater near Selfoss, with the volcano Hekla in the background.

Opposite: *The geyser Strokkur erupts regularly every three to five minutes.*

Most historic sites are usually visited in the whirl-wind day trip known as the **Grand Circle Tour**. It gives a good insight into the scenery and history of Iceland, but it can be rather exhausting and the sites crammed with tourists and coaches. It is far better to take two days and travel independently out of season. Tourist coaches are less obvious in the Reykjanes Peninsula, except at the **Blue Lagoon**, where the waters are known to cure a variety of skin diseases.

Above: *Four-wheel-drive coaches take tourists on the popular Grand Circle Tour from Reykjavík.*
Opposite: *A 'sea-bird city' on the basalt cliffs of Krýsuvíkurberg, located on the southern part of the Reykjanes Peninsula.*

THE REYKJANES PENINSULA

The low peninsula of Reykjanes, just to the south of Reykjavík, juts out into the Atlantic Ocean, facing the full force of the prevailing southwesterly winds. Sitting right on the Mid-Atlantic Ridge, the peninsula is composed largely of lava fields, which are covered with Iceland's ubiquitous grey-green moss. Because of the porous nature of the lava, there are no surface streams and only one lake of any substantial size.

CLIMATE

The weather to the east and south of Reykjavík is quite similar to that in the capital, but the upland in the east attracts higher amounts of both **rain** and **snow**. The Reykjanes Peninsula in the south juts out into the Atlantic Ocean and therefore receives the full force of the prevailing **westerly winds**.

Around Reykjavík

Hafnarfjörður ★

Known as the 'gateway to the Reykjanes Peninsula', Hafnarfjörður, with its population of some 20,000 people, has lately been swallowed up by Greater Reykjavík. However, it is a town in its own right in an administrative sense, having a long history as a trading port, with English merchants controlling the town in the early 15th century, until they were thrown out by the Germans. They, in turn, succumbed to the Danish Trade Monopoly in 1602. The port and fishing industries are still thriving and the town has developed a reputation as a cultural centre. There are a number of museums in Hafnarfjörður, the best being the **Maritime Museum of Iceland**, which is combined with **Hafnarfjörður Folk Museum**, situated at Vesturgata 6–8. It is housed in a 19th-century warehouse appropriately close to the harbour. Open 13:00–17:00 daily in the summer, weekends only in the winter. The **Institute of Culture and Fine Art** at Strandgata 34 stages concerts and exhibitions. It has a pleasant coffee shop with fine harbour views. The highlight in Hafnarfjörður is the annual **Viking Festival** held on the longest day of the year in June. It attracts visitors from all over the world and features strong man competitions, combat exhibitions, folk dancing, longboat trips and traditional Viking foods.

Located immediately to the north of Hafnarfjörður, at the end of the Álftanes Peninsula, is the historic estate of **Bessastaðahreppur**, which is now the official residence of the Icelandic head of state.

To the southeast of Hafnarfjörður, in the centre of the peninsula, is the skiing area of **Bláfjöll** (Blue Mountains). The hills here rise to 702m (2300ft). There are a number of downhill runs and cross-country ski trails, together with chair and rope lifts.

> ### THE LAST GREAT AUK
>
> It is believed that the last pair of great auks were clubbed to death on the island of **Eldey** in 1844. These large, flightless sea birds were very cumbersome on land and therefore easily caught. Their flesh was tasty and for centuries they were an important part of Icelanders' diet. The **Museum of Natural History** in Reykjavík has on display a stuffed great auk, which was obtained at an auction in London in 1971. Meanwhile the great auk's relative, the little auk, survives in small numbers. There are just two pairs left breeding on the island of **Grimsey**. Not surprisingly, they are closely protected.

WHALE-WATCHING FROM KEFLAVÍK

Whale-watching is one of the fastest developing tourist activities and there are plenty of opportunities for visitors in Iceland. Since the ban on whaling, Icelanders are slowly beginning to realize that there is more money to be earned from tourist whaling trips than from commercial fishing for these mammals. A good place to take a trip to see whales is Keflavík, where the **Whale-watching Centre** runs regular tours to observe these fascinating animals at close quarters. The most commonly seen whales are sperm, fin, humpback and minke, while there is also the chance to see seals, dolphins and porpoises, plus a range of sea birds. Be prepared for rough seas!

Reykjanesfólkvangur *

Just to the south of Hafnarfjörður, situated in the centre of the peninsula, is the national nature reserve of Reykjanesfólkvangur, which covers some 775km² (300 sq miles). In amongst the hiking tracks are some amazing lava formations and, in the south of the reserve, a geothermal area known as Krýsuvík, with impressive mud springs, solfataras and steaming vents. In the middle of the reserve is **Lake Kleifavatn**. Its blue waters cover some 10km² (6 sq miles) and it is reputed to be nearly 100m (328ft) deep. Inevitably there are tales of a resident monster. Trout fishing is possible here. At the extreme south of the reserve are the sea-bird cliffs of **Krýsuvíkurberg**. Look for three species of guillemot, kittiwakes, razorbills and, at the top of the cliffs, puffins. The island of **Eldey**, 14km (8.7 miles) offshore, is reputed to be the place where the last great auk was killed. Today Eldey has one of the world's largest gannet colonies.

Right: *Visitors stroll towards the fumeroles, hot springs and geysers of the Krýsuvík geothermal area.*
Opposite: *One of several modern sculptures at Leifur Eiríksson International Airport. Made of aluminium and coloured glass, it represents a rainbow.*

The Western Towns *

The town of Keflavík is a long-established trading port and still has one of the largest fishing fleets in Iceland. It has merged with the neighbouring village of **Njarðvík** to form a settlement of around 10,000 people. Keflavík is best known for being the site of the US-operated NATO base. American troops came here in 1941, replacing British soldiers, with the aim of preventing a German occupation of Iceland. They have remained there ever since, but not without controversy. Keflavík is also the site of the **Leifur Eiríksson International Air Terminal**. The ultramodern building was built with US help and opened in 1987. The airport grounds are noted for their large modern sculptures, which were the result of a competition. Particularly impressive are sculptures of a rainbow and a bird breaking out of an egg.

In the 'toe' of the peninsula are the two somewhat unremarkable fishing villages of **Garður** and **Sandgerði**. Here, some fish processing takes place. Further south is the deserted village of **Bátsendar**, destroyed by a freak wave in 1798. More picturesque is the fishing village of **Hafnir**, midway down the west coast. It has a fine 19th-century wooden church and some restored houses. A 10-minute walk along the cliffs southwards leads to the sea-bird cliffs of **Hafnaberg**.

The only settlement of any size on the south coast of the peninsula is the fishing port of **Grindavík**, which has around 2300 inhabitants. The port has a long trading history and was used by English and German merchants in the late middle ages. One astonishing historical fact

THE NATO BASE

Some 5000 US servicemen are stationed at the Keflavík NATO base, arousing strong opinions among Icelanders. The country has no armed services of its own and many regard the US troops as an occupying army, particularly since the thawing of the Cold War. On the other hand, the US base provides considerable employment. Over 1000 Icelanders work at Keflavik and many more gain an indirect living from the US troops. The NATO forces keep a low profile and are rarely obvious in the towns and countryside.

is that it was raided in 1627 by Algerian pirates, who took away a large number of the local people as slaves. Fish processing and exporting take place here today. Look out for the moving fishermen's monument, called *Hope*, that shows a fisherman's family looking hopefully out to sea.

Above: *Bathing in the medicinal waters of the Blue Lagoon.*
Opposite: *Tomatoes for sale at the roadside. They are grown in geothermally heated greenhouses.*

HEALTH TREATMENT AT THE BLUE LAGOON

The silvery-blue opaque waters of the Blue Lagoon and the white silica mud on its bed have been proven to have great health properties. The cocktail of **minerals** in the water, which comes from up to 1830m (6000ft) below the ground, has eased skin conditions such as psoriasis and eczema. A range of products has been developed, including mineral bath salts, lagoon mud for the face and body, moisturizing cream, and shampoo. Not surprisingly, a complex of facilities opened in 1999 to cope with the 200,000 annual visitors.

The Blue Lagoon (Bláa Lónið) ★★★

Midway between Grindavík and Keflavík is the popular tourist venue known as the Blue Lagoon. The pale blue waters of the Lagoon are in fact the effluent from the Svartsengi power station. Sea water is heated and then filtered as it passes through the lava. The run-off water, which is rich in minerals, has a temperature of 70°C (158°F), but bathing is restricted to one area of the lagoon where temperatures are a more bearable 40°C (104°F). Algae thrive in the hot water, but die as the water cools, adding to the white silica mud on the lake bottom. It sounds unpleasant, but the lagoon water has been shown to relieve the effects of psoriasis, eczema and other skin ailments. There are basic changing rooms, a restaurant and a guesthouse, plus a luxurious touch – swimmers can be served cocktails on floating tables! With steam rising all around and the space-age power equipment and lava fields in the background, a 'swim' in the lagoon can be one of the great tourist experiences of Iceland.

Thorlákshöfn★

In the southeastern corner of the Reykjanes Peninsula is located the **ferry port** of Thorlákshöfn, where regular ferries leave for the **Westmann Islands**. This is the only suitable port in the area between Grindavík and Höfn, which accounts for the long, and often rough, voyage. The ferry boat *Herjólfur* makes a daily return trip to the Westman Islands, weather permitting. The port is named after Saint Thorlákur, who was a bishop of Skálholt during the 12th century and, incidentally, the only Icelander ever to have been canonized by the Roman Catholic church.

East of Reykjavík

The Ring Road (or Route 1) leaves Reykjavík eastwards, running through lava fields and over a mountain pass, before dropping down to the fertile lowland which is one of the country's richest agricultural areas. The first town of any size is **Hveragerði**, with around 1700 inhabitants, many of whom commute daily to the capital. Hveragerði is located on an active geothermal area and several hot springs and steaming vents are readily seen. The geothermal power has been used to heat numerous greenhouses in which crops such as tomatoes, lettuces, cucumbers and flowers are grown. Bananas and other tropical fruits are also produced, but not in a commercial way – just to prove that it can be done! Not surprisingly, Hveragerði is the site of Iceland's National College of Horticulture. There is a small geyser known as Gryta (or Ogress), which erupts several times daily. On the outskirts of the town is a health clinic, with mineral and mud baths, physiotherapy and a health-food shop. Coach tours stop at a tourist trap by the name of **Eden**, based on an old geothermal greenhouse and selling locally grown potted plants, fruits, souvenirs and postcards. The next town along the Ring Road is **Selfoss**, a pleasant market town on the banks of the Ólfusá River. Although it has little of historical interest, Selfoss makes a good centre for exploring the area to the north. Just to the northwest is a hill called **Ingólfsfjall** which

> ### Icelandic Place Names
>
> The majority of Icelandic place names refer to physical or man-made features. If a few of these are understood, it is possible to know something about a place simply by looking at its name on a map. Some of the most common elements are shown below:
>
> *á* • river
> *borg* • rock outcrop
> *brekka* • hillside
> *dalur* • valley
> *ey* • island
> *fell* • hill
> *fjall* • mountain
> *fjörður* • fiord
> *foss* • waterfall
> *gil* • gorge or ravine
> *höfn* • harbour
> *jökull* • icecap or glacier
> *jökulsá* • glacial river
> *mýri* • marsh
> *nes* • peninsula
> *skógur* • woods
> *vatn* • lake
> *vík* • bay

Below: *Turf buildings were largely a response to the lack of timber available.*

rises to a height of 551m (1800ft). The mound on the top is claimed to be the burial site of Ingólfur Arnason, but the summit is solid rock, so this is a doubtful assertion.

From Selfoss, Route 35 leads inland to some of Iceland's most popular tourist locations. After a short distance, on the right-hand side of the road, is the explosion crater of **Kerið**. Some 55m (180ft) deep and enclosing a rather menacing green lake, it was one of a crater swarm formed around 3000 years ago. From here there are distant views of the volcano **Hekla**, its summit usually swathed with cloud. Hekla has erupted at least 20 times since the settlement of Iceland, most recently in 1991.

Skálholt **

The route then leads to the **religious centre** of Skálholt, marked today by a simple, modern church. Its history goes back to the 11th century, when Gissur the White established the first wooden church here. His son, Ísleifur Gissurason, after an education in Germany, became the **first bishop** of Iceland. Skálholt became an important educational centre and an elaborate wooden cathedral replaced the original church. Dark deeds were to come in the 16th century, when the country converted from Catholicism to the Danish Lutheran religion. Bishop **Jón Arason** (who opposed the reformation) and his two sons were beheaded at Skálholt without trial. Today, there is a memorial to Arason on the road leading to the church. The whole site was destroyed during an earthquake in 1784 and shortly afterwards the bishopric was moved to Reykjavík. The present memorial church on the site was built in the 1950s. When the foundations were laid, the remains of the original cathedral were discovered, showing that it was twice the size of the new building. The simple church is worth a visit and is distinguished by some excellent modern stained glass as well as a superb altar mosaic by Nina Tryggvadóttir.

Great Geysir ★★★

From Skálholt, the road leads northeast to the Great Geysir area of **Haukadalur**. Plumes of steam and the sulphurous smell can be noted from some distance away. The Great Geysir is probably the most famous geyser in the world and gave its name to all phenomena of this type. Geysers are spouting hot springs, and the Icelandic word means 'gusher'. The Geysir area covers around 3km² (1.8 sq miles) and consists of geysers, hot springs, mud springs and fumeroles. All have been given Icelandic names. Unfortunately Great Geysir no longer erupts (although eruptions can be induced by throwing soap powder into the crater!), but luckily its neighbour Strokkur ('a churn') is very active, erupting every three to five minutes to a height of around 20m (65ft). The silica crater of Geysir can be inspected, and also some superb blue hot springs nearby. Redeposited silica and travertine surround the spring, and when this material weathers, a wealth of plants and orchids appear. The Great Geysir area has belonged to a number of land-owners, including several Englishmen, one of whom used to charge for admission. In 1935, the land was bought by an Icelandic doctor who then gave it to the nation. There is a convenient hotel nearby, plus a petrol station, cafeteria and camping facilities.

Above: *Unusual religious sculptures carved in stone outside Skálholt's cathedral.*

GEOTHERMAL TERMINOLOGY

Geothermal activity is found in areas of active vulcanicity. The main features are:
Geysers: an explosive spout of hot water
Fumeroles: superheated water turns to steam when the pressure drops as it emerges from the ground.
Solfataras: sulphurous gases escape at the surface, giving the typical 'rotten eggs' smell.
Hot springs: water is heated underground and emerges at the surface.
Mud springs: Hot water mixes with volcanic material and bubbles at the surface.

Right: *The geyser Strokkur begins to erupt. Every three to five minutes clouds of steam and water burst up to 20m (65ft) in height.*
Below right: *Gullfoss – Iceland's best-known waterfall. The name means 'golden falls', named after the rainbow formed by the sun and spray.*

Gullfoss ***

Route 35 continues briefly until Iceland's most famous **waterfall**, Gullfoss, is reached. The name means 'golden falls', after the persistent rainbows which are formed by the spray on sunny days. The **River Hvítá**, swollen by melting snow and ice in the interior, drops some 32m (105ft) over two falls. Above and below Gullfoss is a 2.5km (1.5-mile) gorge up to 70m (230ft) deep. Earlier this century the falls were under threat of hydro-electric development and a local farmer's wife, Sigríður Tómasdóttir, walked all the way to Reykjavík to protest against this, threatening to throw herself down the falls

if the plan went ahead. A memorial to Sigríður stands high above the falls. A footpath from the car park leads down to a viewing platform between the two falls – be sure to take waterproofs as the spray is penetrating.

Laugarvatn *

Southwest of Geysir and Gullfoss is the **spa resort** of Laugarvatn, situated on the shores of a lake of the same name. The name means 'warm lake', and a hot spring nearby called **Vígðalaug** was the traditional place for Christian baptisms by the early bishops of Skálholt. Today, Laugarvatn is an **educational centre**, with a number of colleges which convert to hotels during the summer. The area is a very popular weekend retreat for the inhabitants of Reykjavík, who come for camping, sailboarding and the steam baths.

Thingvellir ***

The Golden Circle Tour's last stop is at Thingvellir, the site of the ancient outdoor parliament, or Althing. The setting is very dramatic, being at the northern end of Thingvallavatn, Iceland's largest lake. It is also right on the Mid-Atlantic Ridge, where the European and North American plates are moving apart. The site is bordered by parallel fissures, namely **Hrafnagjá** in the east and **Almannagjá** in the west. In the early days, the Öxará river was diverted along the Almannagjá to form some rather impressive falls. Just above the bridge over the Öxará is a 'drowning pool' where adulteresses and witches were thrown (delinquent men were usually decapitated). There are numerous historical sites here. The **Lögberg** or 'law rock' on the western side of the

> **RIVER RAFTING**
>
> Iceland is the ideal location for many types of adventure activities. One of the most popular is river rafting. The level can vary from fairly gentle family-style fun to whitewater rafting on rather fearsome glacial rivers and canyons. Strict **safety** is observed with the issue of flotation suits and with training sessions in basic safety and paddling skills. The main sites for rafting are on the river Hvita near Geysir in southern Iceland, near Varmalið in Skagafjörður, and near Egilsstaðir in eastern Iceland. Contact local tourist offices for details.

Below: *Thingvellir – situated on the edge of the 5km-wide fault that divides the American Plate from the European Plate.*

THE DROWNING POOL

Icelandic history is full of grisly stories of murder and dastardly deeds. Its system of justice was often swift and brutal, particularly when it came to the punishment of **women**. At Thingvellir, the **Great Edict of 1564** proclaimed that women found guilty of adultery, infanticide, perjury or, indeed, any other criminal act, would be executed by drowning. At Thingvellir a special pond, the **Drekkingarhylur**, was used for this purpose. The guilty women were tied in a sack before being thrown into the deep 'drowning pond'. This practice, surprisingly, continued until as late as 1838.

Above right: *Thingvellir Historical Site, where the 39 chieftains would meet annually to review the laws of the country.*

river was where the law-speaker was obliged annually to recite the laws of the land from memory. The spot is marked today by a flagpole and plaque. Just east of the Lögberg, on lower ground, was the **Lögretta**, which was the meeting place of the Law Council of 39 chieftains who would discuss new laws. Scattered around the site are the remains of stone *búdir* or **booths** set up by each chieftain for the two-week duration of the Althing. They were used for shelter and as business premises. There are a number of buildings on the site. The **Church** was built in 1859 and is the last of many to have occupied the Althing area. It has a number of relics from past buildings. The cemetery, or **Skáldareitur**, just behind the church, is usually referred to as the 'Poets' Graveyard', although no contemporary poets seem to have selected this as their last resting place. The long **farmhouse** nearby is used as a summer home for the prime minister of Iceland and also contains the offices of the National Park Warden. There are a number of water-filled chasms in the area and one of these, the **Peningagjá**, has developed into a wishing well. Fortunately unobtrusive is the wooden **Hotel Valhöll** on the western side of the river. It occupies the site of Snorri Sturluson's old booth. The region around Thingvellir is excellent hiking country, with number of well-marked trails. It is also possible to drive around the lake on the narrow gravel roads, but traffic can get busy during the summer months.

Around Reykyavík at a Glance

BEST TIMES TO VISIT

The Blue Lagoon is popular all year, and the rest of the area is a summer destination from May–September. Be prepared for crowds at major sites, particularly Gullfoss, Geysir and Thingvellir, in July and August.

GETTING AROUND

Tour coaches and BSÍ buses connect the major sites from June to September, but can be infrequent. The BSÍ Omnibus Pass is available at the BSÍ bus terminal in Reykjavík or at airline offices and travel agents.

WHERE TO STAY

Reykjanes Peninsula
LUXURY
Hótel Keflavík, Vatnsnesvegi 12, 230 Keflavík, tel: 420 7000, fax: 420 7002, e-mail: htkef@ok.is Everything for the air traveller; pool, jacuzzi and sauna; elegant dining room.
Flughotel Icelandais, Hafnargata 57, 230 Keflavík, tel: 421 5222, fax: 421 5223, e-mail: flughotel@icehotel.is There is a nearby golf course.

MID-RANGE
Hótel Bláa Lónið, Svartsengi, 240 Grindavík, tel: 426 8650, fax: 426 8651. Comfortable hotel at Blue Lagoon, with golf course, health facilities and nearby horse rental.
Gistihúsið Kristína, Holtsgata 49, 260 Njarðvík, tel: 421 5622 fax: 421 5648, e-mail: kristina@ok.is Offers free airport transfers.

BUDGET
Youth Hostel Fit, Fitjabraut 6a, tel: 421 8889, fax: 421 8887. Near airport; 50 beds; summer only.
Youth Hostel Strönd, Njarðvíkurbraut 48–50, tel: 421 6211. Both hostels have airport transfers available.
Campsite Keflavík-Njarðvík, tel: 421 1460. Good campsite, open June to mid-September.

East of Reykjavik
MID-RANGE
Hótel Selfoss Icelandair, Eyravegur 2, 800 Selfoss, tel: 482 2500, fax: 482 2524, e-mail: hotel@ka.is Small; has a gourmet restaurant.
Lykilhótel Valhöll, Thingvöllum, 801 Selfoss, tel: 486 1777, fax: 486 1778, e-mail: booking@keyhotel.is Wooden hotel, boats for hire.
Hótel Geysir, Haukadal, 801 Selfoss, tel: 480 6800, fax: 480 6801. Good restaurant.

BUDGET
Gistiheimilið Geysir, Haukadal 111, 801 Selfoss, tel: 486 8733, fax: 872 1573. Basic guesthouse, good value.
HI Youth Hostel, Reykholt, tel: 486 8831, fax: 486 8709. Access to pool and saunas.

CAMPING
Campsites at Geysir, Laugarvatn, Hveragerði, Reyholt, Thingvellir.

WHERE TO EAT

The best (but most expensive) restaurants are in hotels. The restaurants at Keflavík Hotel and Flughótel in Keflavík offer good tourist menus.

Reykjanes Peninsula
MID-RANGE
Jenny by the Blue Lagoon, tel: 426 8650. Restaurant and bistro overlooking the lagoon.
Olsen Olsen, Hafnargata, Keflavík, tel: 421 4457. American 50s-style theme.

BUDGET
Sjómannastofan Vör, Grindavík, tel: 426 8570. Snack bar overlooking the harbour.

East of Reykjavik
MID-RANGE
Lindin, Laugarvatni, tel:486 1262. Restaurant and pizzeria overlooking the lake.

BUDGET
There are good **snack bars** attached to petrol stations at Selfoss and Geysir. Also worth trying are branches of **Pizza 67** in Selfoss and Hveragerði.

USEFUL CONTACTS

Regional Tourist Information Centres: Keflavík Bus Station, tel: 421 5575; Leifur Eiríksson Air Terminal, tel:421 4608; Selfoss, tel: 482 1704; Hveragerði, tel: 483 4280.
Thingvellir National Park Information Service Centre, tel: 482 2660. Information on weather and road conditions in Thingvellir tel: 482 2677.
Thorlákshöfn–Westmann Islands Ferry, tel: 483 3413.

4
West and Northwest Iceland

This chapter covers the region immediately to the north of Reykjavík as far as the Northwest Fiords. This is a region of wide contrasts, both physically and socially. In the south of the area are the two scenically attractive fiords of **Hvalfjörður**, once the centre of Iceland's whaling operations, and **Borgarfjörður**, which is associated with the *Egils Saga*, and the main towns of **Akranes** and **Borganes**. Inland, the village of **Reykholt** has strong links with the 13th-century statesman and writer **Snorri Sturluson**.

The **Snæfellsnes Peninsula** juts out into the ocean and has a number of small fishing settlements scattered around its coastline. At the western end is the icecap of **Snæfellsjökull**, which, on a clear day, can be seen all the way from Reykjavík, 100km (60 miles) away.

The **Northwest Fiords** area is one of the remotest parts of the country. Here most forms of communication between the small, scattered fishing and farming communities are so difficult that light aircraft are commonly used. The region has suffered badly from **depopulation** in recent years, as many of its people have now given up the battle to eke out a living from the harsh landscape and have migrated to Reykjavík. Nevertheless, the wild, uninhabited country of the Northwest Fiords is attractive to hikers in the summer months. Bird-watchers also like to visit the teeming sea-bird cliffs at **Látrabjarg**, the most westerly point in Europe, and **Hornstradir** in the north. The inhospitable climate, however, ensures that tourists are rare birds themselves!

TOP ATTRACTIONS

** **Reykholt:** associated with 13th-century statesman and writer Snorri Sturluson.
** **Sea-bird cliffs:** at Látrabjarg and Hornstradir in the Northwest Fiords.
** **Ísafjörður:** town with good fiord location and Iceland's best maritime museum.
* **Snæfellsjökull:** snow-capped volcano at west end of the Snæfellsnes Peninsula.
** **Hraunfossar and Barnafoss Falls:** unusual waterfalls in the upper reaches of the Hvítá valley.

Opposite: *Sugandafjörður, an example of the stunning scenery in the remote northwest fiords of Iceland.*

HVALFJÖRÐUR AND BORGARFJÖRÐUR

North of Reykjavík, the Ring Road runs seaward around **Mount Esja**, some 918m (3011ft) high, before swinging around into **Hvalfjörður**. The name means 'whale fiord' and this was the centre of Icelandic whaling operations until the country's withdrawal from the industry in 1992. Whales are frequently seen in the fiord today and some 17 species have been recorded here. The deep waters of Hvalfjörður were ideal for British and American warships in World War II, and the remains of the base can be seen on the north side of the fiord. Equally unattractive is the ferro silicon smelter at Grundartangi, near the mouth of the fiord. On the north side is the delightful little church at **Saurbær**, built in memory of Hallgrímur Pétursson, who in the 17th century composed Iceland's best-known religious work, *50 Passion Hymns*.

Akranes ★★★

One of Iceland's largest fishing ports, the town of Akranes, with a population of just over 5500, is located right on the very tip of the peninsula which separates Hvalfjörður and Borgarfjörður. The town is dominated by the chimneys of its cement works, which uses local basalt and shell sand. Akranes can be reached by the new road tunnel across the mouth of Hvalfjörður, which

Below: *Inshore fishing boats. Most of the coastal villages in the northwest of Iceland depend on fishing for their income.*

has cut the journey from Reykjavík by about 60km (37 miles), or alternatively by regular ferry services from the capital. The main attraction at Akranes is the **Regional Folk and Maritime Museum** at Garðar just to the east of the town. There are indoor and outdoor exhibits, including *Sigurfari*, an old 19th-century decked cutter, and also numerous whaling artefacts. Outside the museum is a stone tower with inscriptions in both Icelandic and Gaelic. It was a gift from the people of Ireland in 1974, commemorating the 1100th anniversary of the Settlement and Akranes's original Irish immigrants who founded the town around AD880.

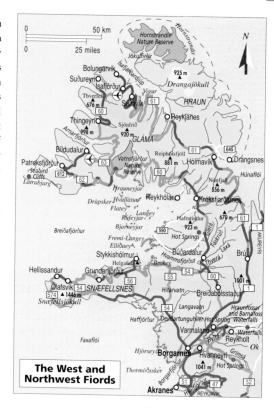

The West and Northwest Fiords

Borganes ***

Situated halfway along the northern side of Borgar-fjörður, Borganes is quite unusual in that it is perhaps the only coastal town in Iceland that doesn't specialize in fishing. Instead, it is a service centre for the inland area. Borganes has a small folk museum (open daily in summer, 14:00–18:00), but most visitors head for the small park. Here is a burial mound, said to be that of Skalla-grímmur Kveldúlfsson, the father of Egill Skallagrímsson of *Egils Saga* fame. It is said that Egill carried the body of his drowned son to be buried next to his grandfather – a touching tale that is depicted on a relief plaque made by the Danish artist Annemarie Brodersen.

THE UBIQUITOUS LUPIN

In mid-June the countryside is covered with wild flowers. One of the most noticeable is the **Alaskan Lupin** (*Lupinus nootkatensis*) which grows in blue swathes. This is no ordinary wild flower, for being a leguminous plant, it adds nitrogen to the soil. Its root system also binds the soil together and helps to prevent erosion, which has proved useful on the *sandur* in south Iceland.

Reykholt ***

This small hamlet to the west of Borganes is one of Iceland's most important historical sites. It was the home of **Snorri Sturluson**, the famous 13th-century Saga writer and statesman. Snorri lived at Reykholt from 1206–1241 and wrote many of his best works here. Today, we can see the thermal pool where Snorri bathed and the nearby tunnel which connected with the farm where he lived. The tunnel probably led to the cellar where he was murdered by his enemies in 1241, at the age of 62.

The modern church has a cultural centre where some of his work is on display. In front of the school is a statue of the writer by Norwegian sculptor Gustav Vigeland. It was a gift from Norway in gratitude for one of Snorri's most famous works, *Heimskringla*, a Saga featuring the kings of medieval Norway. In the cemetery of the older church is a gravestone marked *Sturlingareitur*, and it is possible that this might be Storri's last resting place. Also of interest in the Reykholt valley is the country's most powerful hot spring, known as **Deildartunguhver**. It spurts out water at 200 litres (352 pints) per second at a temperature of 100°C (212°F). Not surprisingly, a greenhouse industry has developed here and fresh produce is often on sale at the roadside. The hot water is piped some 60km (37 miles) to supply both Borkanes and Akranes.

Inland from Reykholt *

To the east of the Ring Road and to the west of the Langjökull icecap is an area, full of geological interest, which is known as **Húsafell**. It can also be approached by a scenic road from Thingvellir, though this route is only likely to be open during July and August. To the east of Husafell are extensive lava sheets which include the **Hallmundarhraun Caves**. These feature a series of tubes within the lava; the longest, known as Surtshellir,

---

THE FORMIDABLE SNORRI

The life of the 13th-century Icelandic writer and diplomat Snorri Sturluson was as full of intrigue and violence as any of the Sagas. Born in 1179, he married an heiress at the age of 21, and liaisons with other wealthy women ensured that he became the richest man in Iceland. He mainly lived and worked on a large estate at Reykholt where he wrote his greatest works. He became law-speaker of the Althing at the age of 36. He developed a close relationship with the King of Norway. Later that relationship soured and the King demanded Snorri's return to Norway. Snorri ignored his request and in 1241 he was assassinated at Reykholt by Gissur Thorvaldsson, a rival chieftain hoping to impress the King of Norway. Snorri left behind a formidable collection of literature, including the *Prose Edda*, *Heimskringla* and, in all probability, *Egils Saga*.

is some 4km (2½ miles) in length. The caves have the usual stalactites and stalagmites, and occasional large caverns. Visitors should bring a torch, as there is no artificial lighting. West of Husafell are the **Hraunfossar Falls**, where the glacial River Hvítá has created a gorge over 1km (0.6 mile) in length. The sides of the gorge have a long string of springs which emerge from the junction of porous rock and basalt. A track leads upstream to **Barnafoss** ('children's waterfall'), named after children who, while on their way to church, fell from a natural rock arch over the falls and were drowned.

THE SNÆFELLSNES PENINSULA

Running east–west and jutting out into the ocean, the Snæfellsnes Peninsula receives the full force of Atlantic gales. The population, not surprisingly, is sparse here. The south coast of the peninsula has a broad coastal plain, but lacks good harbours. Consequently there are no townships of any size, just a scattering of farmsteads. A mountain chain runs along the centre of the peninsula, rising to approximately 930m (3050ft) at **Tröllatindar**. The highest mountain, however, is **Snæfellsjökull**, at 1446m (4745ft), at the western end of the peninsula. It is a conically shaped dormant volcano with three distinct peaks, covered by a small icecap which can frequently be seen from Reykjavík, some 100km (60 miles) to the south. In Jules Verne's story *Journey to the Centre of the Earth*, the explorers began their journey at Snæfellsjökull, emerging sometime later at Stromboli volcano in Italy! Snæfellsjökull can be climbed by three different routes, which each take about four to five hours to complete and which demand the use of equipment such as crampons and ice axes. There are also snowmobile routes to the summit. Always be prepared for the worst possible weather.

GRAVEL ROADS

The surface of many roads in Iceland (even parts of the Ring Road) is composed of gravel. This brings great hazards to the motorist. When two cars are passing, drivers are advised to **slow down**, as projectile stones may shatter windscreens. The shoulders of gravel roads can be quite soft and drivers must be careful not to allow their outside wheels to skid in this material. There are not always road signs to indicate the change from an asphalted road to a gravel road. Take care in summer, when the dust raised by a passing car can obscure visibility for some time.

Opposite: *Snorri's Pool, Reykholt. Here the statesman and Saga writer Snorri Sturluson lived and died.*
Below: *At Hraunfossar a line of waterfalls emerges from a rock junction in the side of the gorge.*

Below: *Sunset across Breiðafjörður, a lovely wide island-studded bay marking the start of the northwest fiord area. Ferries from Stykkishólmur regularly cross the bay.*

Stykkishólmur ★★★

The largest town on Snæfellnes Peninsula, Stykkishólmur has a long history and many connections with the Sagas. In the early days it was a religious centre. The nearby hill of **Helgafell** (or Holy Mountain) has always been considered to have supernatural powers and also figures strongly in local folklore. Today Stykkishólmur is a trading and fishing port, specializing in shellfish. Close to the harbour is a folk museum called the **Norwegian House**, which was brought from Norway in 1828 by Árni Thorlacius (who also made Iceland's first meteorological measurements at Stykkishólmur in 1845). The museum is open from 15:00–18:00 on weekdays and 11:00–18:00 on weekends. Stykkishólmur's most striking building, however, is its new **Roman Catholic Church**. Built on a headland and made of concrete, it soars skywards in gentle curves. The car ferry *Baldur* makes regular trips from Stykkishólmur across Breiðafjörður to Brjánslækur in the Northwest Fiords. Breiðafjörður is littered with over 2000 small islands, and the ferry stops at one of these, named **Flatey**. Once a religious and cultural centre, few people live on Flatey today, although many city dwellers have holiday homes here. The island houses Iceland's smallest and oldest library.

Left: *Looking towards Drangajökull from near Suðavík. Drangajökull is the only permanent icecap in the northwest.*

Elsewhere on the Snæfellsnes Peninsula ★★★

There are a number of other fishing settlements along the north coast of the peninsula. The most westerly is **Ólafsvík**, Iceland's longest established trading port, having been given its charter in 1687. There is a small folk museum based in an old packing house. Further east is **Grundarfjörður**, surrounded by forbidding mountains. In the early 19th century it was used as a base by French fishermen, who built a church here. The northeastern part of the peninsula is marked by the broad **Hvammsfjörður**. The coastal village of **Búðardalur** is the main service centre for the region. Inland is the narrow **Laxárdalur Valley**, famous as the site of the *Laxdæla Saga*, a popular Icelandic love story. Several famous Icelanders were born in Laxádalur, including the writer Snorri Sturluson, the discoverer of America, Leifur Eiríksson, and the heroine of the *Laxdæla Saga*, Guðrún Ösvífursdóttir.

THE NORTHWEST FIORDS

Northwest Iceland is one of the most inhospitable parts of the country. Geologically, this is the oldest part of Iceland, with basalt rocks some 50 million years old. It was one of the most recent areas to be glaciated and has a large surviving icecap, called **Drangajökull**, which covers about 175 km² (109 sq miles). The high interior, known as **Gláma**, is a tundra plateau, with thin rocky soil, moraines and lakes. The ice, which has only recently

> ### SORTING OUT YOUR GUILLEMOTS
>
> Guillemots are easily recognized as black-and-white diving sea birds belonging to the **auk** family. They have a 'whirring' flight and an upright stance on land. In Iceland, however, identification is complicated by the fact that there are **three** species of guillemots. The most widely seen is the **common guillemot**, which is found throughout the northeast Atlantic. Rarer is the **black guillemot** which, as its name suggests, is black all over (except for white patches on its wings and bright red legs). The third species sends bird-watchers into raptures – this is **Brünnich's guillemot**, distinguished by a narrow white line stretching back from the eye and seen only with binoculars. The common and Brünnich's guillemots are cliff-nesters, but the black guillemot prefers bank holes.

Above: *The small settlement of Mýrar, which nestles on the north side of Dýrafjörður.*
Below: *The rugged scenery of the northwest highlands is formed by some of the oldest rocks in the country.*

FEATHERED NOMADS

One of the world's most remarkable nomadic birds, the **Arctic Tern** (*Sterna paradisæa*), is, in fact, very common in Iceland. The bird summers in northern sub-Arctic regions where it breeds, but in the northern winter it flies over 17,000km (10,500 miles) to the Antarctic. Arctic terns are regarded with special affection by the Icelanders, as their arrival is seen as the harbinger of spring. The birds can be less affectionate at their nesting sites, however, and will 'dive bomb' any intruders, including human beings, who are well advised to wear head protection.

---

left, has carved out deep, steep-sided coastal fiords, making this region the most scenically attractive in Iceland. The climate, though, is harsh, with piercing Arctic winds and heavy snowfalls in winter. Farming is extremely difficult and many parts have become abandoned. Communications are problematic too. Remote from the Ring Road, northwest coastal roads are badly surfaced and wind around fiords, making journeys long and arduous. Public transport by road is infrequent, but there are a few ferries, particularly in Ísafjarðardjúp. The only sustainable work in the area is **fishing**. The warm Gulf Stream and cold Greenland Current meet offshore, providing good spawning conditions for fish. There are also sheltered harbours aplenty. Unfortunately, Government quotas on the fish caught have resulted in many fishermen leaving. There are, however, many attractions for the tourist in summer. For hikers, there are numerous marked trails amongst wilderness scenery, while for bird watchers, the northwest holds some of the finest sea-bird cliffs in the world.

Ísafjörður***

The largest settlement in the Northwest Fiords area is Ísafjörður, which has around 4000 inhabitants. It has one of the most dramatic locations of any town in Iceland,

situated on a narrow sand spit jutting out into the fiord, its steep sides cloaked with scree slopes and, at upper levels, hanging valleys left by glaciers. Ísafjörður has a long history as a trading port and today has an important fishing industry. It also acts as the cultural and commercial centre of the Northwest Fiords. Regular flights to Ísafjörður from Reykjavík have helped develop a modest tourist trade, but due to its remoteness and poor infrastructure, it will never be swamped with visitors.

A number of 18th-century wooden houses have survived on the end of the sand spit. Today these house the **Westfjörds Maritime Museum** which is full of old photographs, nautical artefacts and fishing implements. The star exhibit is a reproduction of an early six-oared sailing ship. Open from 13:00–17:00 during summer.

There are several ferries which double as fiord sightseeing boats, including the *Fagranes,* which cruises the Ísafjarðardjúp, stopping on request. Its ports of call include the islands of Vigur and Ædey (Eider Island), both of which are noted for their bird life. *Fagranes* also visits **Hornstrandir**, in the northernmost tip of the Northwest Fiords. This wilderness area is now uninhabited and is designated as a nature reserve, typified by sheer sea cliffs, glaciated valleys and rugged mountains. The arctic fox thrives here, and whales and seals are often seen offshore. In the absence of grazing sheep, the wild flowers are spectacular. Most impressive of all are the sea-bird cliffs, which rise vertically in places to over

THE WHALING ISSUE

Iceland has a long tradition of whaling and has been at loggerheads with environmental agencies such as Greenpeace for some years. In 1992, Iceland withdrew from the **International Whaling Commission (IWC)**, claiming that it had been taken over by 'radicals'. In doing so, it forfeited its right to catch its annual 'scientific quota' of 400 whales and, at the time of writing, whaling is non-existent in Iceland. The country claims, however, that numbers of minke and fin whales have recovered sufficiently for whaling to resume, although the IWC disagrees with this viewpoint. Meanwhile, Icelanders have begun to realize that there is just as much money to be made from whale-watching as a tourist activity as there is from commercial whaling.

Left: *An eider duck sits on her nest in the remote Dýrafjörður area of northwest Iceland.*

Above: *The reflections of Dvergarsternsofell in the waters of Álftafjörður in northwest Iceland.*

500m (1650ft). Guillemots, puffins, razorbills, kittiwakes and fulmars breed in profusion, while there is always the possibility of seeing the rare white-tailed sea eagle. Note that there is no accommodation in the Hornstrandir area apart from mountain huts.

An hour's excursion by boat from Ísafjörður leads to **Vigur Island**. In this pristine environment there are only 11 inhabitants, but thousands of tame seabirds nesting on the grassy slopes. There is a tearoom, post office and the only eider duck feather factory in Iceland.

Around the Northwest Fiords ***

Other coastal settlements of note include **Suðavík**, once a Norwegian whaling station, the geothermal centre of **Reykjanes**, and **Suðureyri**, which is in the unenviable position of having no direct sunlight for four months of the year. The most westerly point in Europe is marked by the lighthouse at **Látrabjarg**. To the south of this are the **Látrabjarg Cliffs**, which are 12km (7½ miles) long and rise to over 500m (1650ft). In summer the ledges of the cliffs teem with breeding sea birds, including puffins, guillemots, fulmars and cormorants. There is also an estimated one third of the world's razorbills nesting here. The local people are accomplished at abseiling down the cliffs to collect birds' eggs, a skill that came in useful in 1947, when a British trawler ran aground at the foot of the cliffs. The local farmers casually saved the entire crew by hauling them up the 200m (650ft) cliffs by rope, even stopping half-way up, it is said, to give them soup!

West and Northwest Iceland at a Glance

BEST TIMES TO VISIT

The south of this region can be visited for most of the year. The further north you go, however, the more hostile the winter climate becomes. The chilling Arctic winds and the poor surfaces of most of the roads in the Northwest Fiords area make this a summer venue.

GETTING THERE

The Ring Road goes through the southern part of this area, which is also well served by a number of scheduled bus routes. However, access is more difficult in the region of the Snæfellsnes Peninsula, and particularly in the Northwest Fiords. The ferry *Akraborg* runs at least four times a day between Reykjavík and Akranes. The ferry *Baldur* plies the route between Stykkishólmur on the Snæfellsnes Peninsula and Brjánslækur on the south side of the Northwest Fiords. From there it is a circuitous drive to anywhere else in the area. Air travel is convenient. Flights run from Reykjavík to Thingreyri, Stykkishólmur, Patreksfjörður, Flateyri, and Ísafjörður.

GETTING AROUND

Travelling in the Snæfellsnes Peninsula and the Northwest Fiords is difficult in winter when heavy snowfall can cause problems on the road. Many of the bus services in the region only run in summer, and even then careful planning is essential.

WHERE TO STAY

In the remoter areas of the west, few hotels are open all year, and in summer they can quickly become booked up. Forward planning is advisable.

MID-RANGE

Hótel Borganes, Egilsgata 14–16, 310 Borganes, tel: 437 1119, fax: 437 1443, e-mail: hotelbo@centrum.is Summer hotel; good restaurant.
Hótel Barbró, Kirkjubraut 11, 300 Akranes, tel: 431 4240, fax: 431 4241, e-mail: barbro @aknet.is Has a pool and restaurant. Golf course nearby.
Hótel Stykkishólmur, Vatnsás, 340 Stykkishólmur, tel: 430 2100, fax: 430 2101, e-mail: hotelstykkisholmer@ simnet.is Has a restaurant, and there are bikes for hire.
Hótel Ísafjörður, Silfurtorg 2, 400 Ísafjörður, tel: 456 4111, fax: 456 4767. Summer hotel; good restaurant. Cheaper annexe nearby. Open all year.

BUDGET

Budget accommodation available in hostels and campsites. There are a number of **HI hostels** in the area, namely at Patreksfjörður, Borganes, Reykholt and Stykkishólmur

(the latter is one of Iceland's best hostels). There are also several excellent **campsites**, including those at Borganes, Ólafsvík and Ísafjörður.

WHERE TO EAT

High-class restaurants are somewhat few and far between in this part of the country, and frequently the restaurants in the hotels are the only available choice for dining. Particularly well recommended are the restaurant at the **Hótel Ísafjörður**, which has a very good tourist menu, and the one at the **Hótel Borganes**.

USEFUL CONTACTS

There are **Tourist Information Centres** at the following places:
Akranes: Skólabraut 31, tel: 431 3327.
Borganes: at the Esso petrol station, tel: 437 2108.
Stykkishólmur: Aðalgata 2, tel: 438 1150.
Ísafjörður: Aðelstræti 7, tel: 438 1450.
Vesturfirðir: the tourist office is at Ísafjörður, tel: 456 5121, and offers a variety of boat cruises and hiking excursions in the vicinity.

STYKKISHÓLMUR	J	F	M	A	M	J	J	A	S	O	N	D
AVE. TEMP. °C	-1.8	-0.7	-0.8	1.6	4.9	8.1	9.9	9.6	6.7	3.9	0.9	-0.8
AVE. TEMP. °F	28.7	30.7	30.5	34.9	40.8	46.6	49.8	49.3	44	39	33.6	30.5
AVE. RAINFALL mm	67.5	68.9	71.7	52.9	33.7	40.2	42.1	51.7	56.6	80.3	66.8	71.6
AVE. RAINFALL in	2.66	2.71	2.82	2.08	1.33	1.58	1.62	2.04	2.23	3.16	2.63	2.82

5
Northern Iceland

After the Reykjavík area, Northern Iceland is the part of the country which is most popular among tourists. It has many attractions, not the least of which is the weather. Despite being only a stone's throw away from the Arctic Circle (which straddles the offshore island of Grímsey), summers can be pleasantly warm and much drier than in the south of the country. Pastoral farming thrives in the lowland areas.

The coastline is marked by a series of rugged peninsulas protruding into the Arctic Ocean, with fiords, bays and occasional river deltas. Some of the inland areas have been heavily glaciated, leaving spectacular mountain scenery. The eastern part of the area lies on the plate boundary, and in the **Lake Mývatn** area there are numerous volcanic features, such as **Krafla** volcano, lava flows, pseudo craters and mud springs. In the extreme east is a largely unpopulated, gravel-strewn, cold desert, almost totally devoid of vegetation. Hikers head for the attractive **Jökulsárgljúfur National Park**, where a long gorge has been formed by glacial meltwaters. Numerous waterfalls can be seen here, including the imposing **Dettifoss**, said to be the most powerful falls in Europe. Bird-watchers are in their element in this part of Iceland, with Lake Mývatn a major attraction. Huge numbers of duck breed in this shallow lake, which is fed by warm underground springs.

The Ring Road bisects Northern Iceland and most of the important settlements can be found along its route. Dominating the area is **Akureyri**, the country's second

---

DON'T MISS

*** Lake Mývatn Area: teeming bird life and the country's most spectacular volcanic features.
*** Jökulsárgljúfur National Park: Iceland's own version of the Grand Canyon, with the powerful Dettifoss waterfall.
*** Glaumbær Folk Museum: take a look inside a turf farm complex.
** Húsavík: superb whale-watching from this northern fishing port.
** Goðafoss: the accessible 'Waterfall of the Gods'.

Opposite: *Turf huts at the Glaumbær Folk Museum to the south of Sauðárkrókur.*

largest town and the regional and service centre for the whole of Northern Iceland. It has a university, a clutch of interesting museums and some fine botanical gardens. It is also the main air and sea port of the area. A number of small fishing ports are scattered around the coastline, including **Húsavík**, which has become quite well known for its whale-watching tours.

Above: *Whale-watching tours from Húsavík are likely to be rewarded with photographs such as this tail fin of a breaching sperm whale.*

CLIMATE

The north of Iceland has a more continental climate than the south, with drier, sunnier summers, but colder winters and more snowfall. Rainfall is light, but northerly winds can bring very cold conditions. This is the most sunny part of the country, but the wind-chill factor is high. The temperature in Akureyri averages 2.4°C (27.5°F) in **January** and 10.7°C (51°F) in **July**, with an average total **rainfall** of 470mm (18.5 in).

THE WEST OF THE REGION

The Ring Road joins the area at the small settlement of **Brú** at the head of the narrow **Hrútafjörður**. This leads out into the wide bay of **Húnaflói**. The word translates as 'Bear Bay', named, no doubt, after the many Greenland bears which have washed ashore here on ice floes. The Ring Road now heads to the northeast, with distant views of the moraine-dammed salt-water lagoon of **Hóp**, where seals can often be seen basking on the sand at low tide.

The first settlement of any size is **Blönduós**, situated on both banks of the River Blandaá, a popular (and expensive) salmon river. Blönduós is dominated by its church – a modern concrete affair clearly designed in the shape of a volcanic crater. The only other feature to detain visitors is the small handicraft museum, which is open weekdays from 14:00–17:00. North of Blönduós is the rugged and remote **Skagi Peninsula**. The only settlement of importance here is the old trading centre and current fishing port of **Skagaströnd**. A gravel road runs around the perimeter of the peninsula. The northerly point is marked by an unmanned lighthouse, and nearby are some remarkable ledges of horizontal basalt.

From here the Ring Road heads inland over some superb glacial scenery, before dropping right down into the Héradsvötn valley and the little settlement of **Varmahlíð**, which is currently growing as a service centre for the surrounding area.

Saudárkrókur ***

Located at the head of Skagafjördur, Saudárkrókur, with a population of around 2600, is the second largest town in the north of Iceland. Its position 25km (15.5 miles) north of the Ring Road means that it does not see as many tourists as it deserves. The town developed on the site of an old trading post, and its industries include fish processing and the making of fibreglass. There is a small **Art and Folk Museum**, which includes one of the few blacksmith's forges in Iceland. There are hiking possibilities in the mountains behind the town. Boat trips are offered to the island of **Drangey** in Skagafjördur, where the steep cliffs house thousands of breeding sea birds. Both the birds and their eggs have been a rich source of food for local people in the past.

> ### THE ARCTIC FOX
>
> Iceland's only native land mammal is the **arctic fox** (*Alopex lagopus*). Greyish brown in summer, in winter it grows a thick, furry coat that turns much lighter, almost white. It is well-insulated and may even grow fur on its paws. The arctic fox was common throughout the country, but because farmers thought it killed lambs, it has been persecuted and has retreated to less habited areas. In fact, it poses little threat to healthy sheep and largely exists on small birds, eggs, fish and shellfish, though it will feed on carcasses of sheep and dead sea birds. There have been attempts to **breed** foxes on fur farms, but these animals have generally been brought in from abroad.

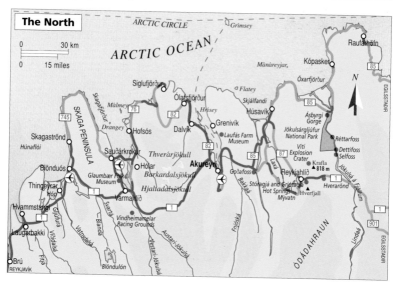

CONSERVATION AWARENESS IN ICELAND

It has to be said that conservation awareness in Iceland is low. Historically, the population has always been small and mainly confined to the coastal regions. There seemed little reason, therefore, to worry about the vast expanse of wilderness in the interior. The second half of the 20th century saw the growth of urban areas and the widespread use of four-wheel-drive vehicles, which gave the town-dwellers easy access to wilderness areas. Such regions are badly in need of protection. There are few voluntary environmental organizations, however, and conservation bills seem to attract little interest in the Icelandic parliament. Fortunately, it is gradually dawning on the authorities that Iceland has the potential to become one of the great **eco-tourism** destinations in the world. The sensitive sites, however, need urgent protection.

South of Sauðárkrókur★★★

The Héradsvötn River has built up a sizeable delta at the head of Skagafjörður. Although it is rich farmland, it is prone to flooding when snows melt in early summer. Above the flood plain to the west is the **Glaumbær Folk Museum**, based on an 18th-century turf farm. It consists of a complex of small separate buildings linked by a central passageway. The buildings include guest rooms, a dairy, a pantry, a kitchen and living rooms (or *baðstofa*). It was in the latter that the work of the farmhouse took place. The women of the house would weave and spin, while the men combed wool and made ropes. A member of the household would usually read a Saga or recite poetry while the others worked. The *baðstofa* also contained beds, and many people would sleep together for warmth. The rooms are full of fascinating artefacts from previous centuries. Glaumbær is also the burial place of Snorri Thorfinasson, who is believed to have been the first European to be born in North America. This was in the year 1003, when his parents went on an expedition to Vinland. The museum, which is open daily, 09:00–18:00 from June to September, is highly recommended. There is a small café in a nearby building.

Iceland horse enthusiasts will certainly wish to visit the **Vindheimamelar Racing Grounds**, approximately 10km (6 miles) south of Varmahlíð. An audiovisual

Left: *Icelandic horses show their paces at the Vindheim-amelar Racing Grounds.*
Opposite: *The Glaumbær Folk Museum is on an 18th-century turf farm.*

presentation is followed by a demonstration of the five gaits of this hardy breed. Refreshments are provided, but reservations are necessary.

Hólar ★★★

Another diversion to the north of Varmahlíð along the eastern side of the Heraðsvötn valley eventually leads to the **religious centre** of Hólar. This was the northern bishopric in Iceland from 1106 until the Reformation. The first wooden cathedral here was built from Norwegian timber, and for a century it was the world's largest wooden church. In 1798, the bishop's seat was abolished, and the site later became an **agricultural college**. The present church at Hólar dates from 1757 and is made of the local red sandstone. The bell tower contains the remains of the first Bishop, Jón Ögmundarson who, together with his son, was executed at Skálholt for his opposition to Danish reforms. The interior of the church is full of interest and well worth a visit. Climb the tower for spectacular views. There are guided tours between 14:00 and 18:00 daily.

Akureyri

Located at the head of Eyjafjörður, the fast-growing town of Akureyri is the 'capital' of Northern Iceland and one of the country's most pleasant urban areas. Akureyri became a trading centre in the early 17th century, but it was over 100 years later that the first people lived here.

> ### The Remarkable Icelandic Horse
>
> Despite the small size of the Icelandic horse, please don't ever call it a pony! Behind its small but sturdy frame is a remarkable animal. It is a **pure-bred** horse, found in a variety of colours, and unique in having **five gaits**. In addition to the usual walk, trot and gallop, it has the tölt and the pace, the latter two giving a smooth, comfortable ride for the equestrian. This singular horse is a very valuable animal and is exported throughout the world. A hardy animal, it is also a good **workhorse**, and up to the start of the 20th century it was essential for transport and farm work. Furthermore, its toughness meant that it was quite happy to spend the winter outdoors. Today, the Icelandic horse is largely used for **sport** and **recreation**.

Above: *The harbour at Akureyri, where there is an important fish canning and freezing industry.*

Its main growth has taken place during the 20th century. It now has a population of around 15,000. Akureyri has always specialized in fish products, and herring salting was initially important. After the stocks declined, the emphasis turned to the canning and freezing of larger fish such as cod. Other industries include food processing, brewing and, increasingly, tourism. A number of old wooden buildings have been preserved in the town, and its residents take great pride in their gardens, which means that the town has a pleasant cared-for feel. There is an attractive central shopping mall and numerous bookshops, libraries, churches and museums. The riverside is full of interest, with fishing and cargo boats, families of harlequin and eider ducks, and planes flying low down the fiord to land at the airport.

Akureyrarkirkja *

The parish church sits high on the hill overlooking the town centre and is well worth the climb. This modern church has rather a 'geological' appearance, and it is not really surprising to learn that it was designed by the same architect who was responsible for the Hallgrímskirkja in Reykjavík. It is worth looking at the interior – the central chancel window came from the old Coventry Cathedral in the UK, somehow surviving the blitz. The ship hanging from the ceiling is an old Norse tradition meant to protect seafarers.

Museums ***

Akureyri has an extraordinary number of museums. Many of these are small affairs celebrating former sons of the town and will be of minimal interest to the foreign visitor, but others are well worth a visit.

THE ARCTIC OPEN

One of Iceland's current obsessions is **golf** and an increasing number of golf courses are appearing around the country. Although conditions in winter are not very suitable for the game, the long summer days are ideal. The golf course at **Jaðarsvöllur**, just to the southwest of Akureyri, provides the venue for Iceland's best-known competition, the 36-hole Arctic Open, which is played throughout the night in late June. Visitors wishing to play will find, however, that there is a handicap limit and a hefty registration fee.

The **Natural History Museum** at Hafnarstræti 81 contains a comprehensive collection of eggs, mammals, insects, flora and stuffed birds. The star exhibit is a mock-up of the extinct Great Auk, the parts having been put together from other birds. Open 10:00–17:00 Jun–Sep.

The fascinating **Akureyri Folk Museum** displays an interesting collection of both household and workplace artefacts dating back to the time of the Settlement. Situated at Aðalstræti 58, this museum is open from 11:00–17:00 daily, Jun–Sep.

Nonnahús is the childhood home of the Reverend Jón Sveinnsson (1857–1944), who was nicknamed 'Nonni'. He wrote a number of works for children, based on his own youthful experiences. The building is a revealing example of the cramped conditions people lived in during the 19th century in Iceland. Sveinnsson's statue dominates the garden. The house is open from 11:00–17:00 daily, Jun–Sep.

Laxdalshús, at Hafnarstræti 11, is the oldest building in Akureyri, dating from 1795. It functioned originally as a Danish trading house. An excellent audiovisual display traces the history of the town. It is open from 11:00–17:00 daily, Jun–Sep.

There are also small museums celebrating the work of Davið Stefánsson and Matthías Jochumsson, both of whom became Icelandic poets laureate.

> **AKUREYRI'S FAVOURITE SON**
>
> The Reverend **Jón Sveinsson** (1857–1944), who was also known as 'Nonni', lived in Akureyri as a child before being educated in France, Denmark and England. He was ordained as a **Jesuit priest** and taught in Denmark for many years, but ill health forced him into an early retirement and he turned to writing **children's stories**, many of which referred back to his own childhood in Iceland. He wrote in German, but his books have been translated into nearly 50 different languages. Many of his original works can be seen in his former home, **Nonnahús**, in Akureyri.

Below: *Akureyri Church, designed by the architect responsible for the Hallgríms-kirkja in Reykjavík.*

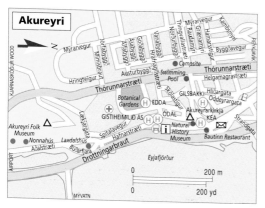

Visitors should not leave Akureyri without visiting
the **Botanical Gardens**. The gardens were founded in
1912 by the local townswomen and were then taken over
by the local authority in 1955. There is a comprehensive
collection of Icelandic plants, all carefully labelled, plus
a number of different plants from all around the world.
It is amazing to find Mediterranean plants surviving at
this high latitude. The Botanical Gardens are open from
08:00–22:00, June to September.

NORTH OF AKUREYRI

There are a number of small ports north of Akureyri. On
the eastern side of Eyjafjörður is **Grenivík**, which has a
large fish-freezing plant. Just to the south is the **Laufás
Farm Museum**, based on an old turf farmhouse dating
from 1850. On the opposite side of the fiord is the ferry
port of **Dalvík**. Its main claim to fame is the 1934
earthquake which measured 6.3 on the Richter Scale
and destroyed half the town. Ferries leave Dalvík for
Grímsey, calling en route at the island of Hrísey in
the middle of the fiord. Further north is the port of
Ólafsfjörður, which is considered to have one of the
most attractive settings in the country. It is now reached
by a 3.5km (2-mile) tunnel through the surrounding
peaks. At the northern end of the peninsula lies the
fishing port of **Sigulfjörður**, located in a short but

Right: *The northern fishing port of Húsavík has
become the whale-watching
capital of Iceland since
commercial whaling ceased.*

Left: *A short walk from the Ring Road, Goðafoss is Iceland's most accessible waterfall. The name means 'Waterfall of the Gods'.*

spectacular fiord. It was originally named Thormóðseyri after Thormóður the Strong, who was the first settler. Sigulfjörður was the third largest town in Iceland during the years of the herring boom. The town declined with the herring, but the golden years are remembered in the harbourside Herring Museum. Open 10:00–18:00 daily.

Goðafoss ★★★

The Ring Road leaves Akureyri eastwards and follows the far shore of the fiord, giving superb views across to the town. It then climbs the mountains through superb glacial scenery before dropping down into the next valley, that of the River Skjálfandaflót. Just a short stroll from the road is Goðafoss, Iceland's most accessible **waterfall**, formed as the river cuts into a lava field. The name means 'Waterfall of the Gods', a title which dates back to AD1000 when the law-speaker, Thorgeir, was returning from the Althing. The parliament had just decided to adopt the Christian religion, and Thorgeir decided that the falls would be a good place to dispose of his pagan idols.

Húsavík ★★★

From the road junction at nearby Laugar, Route 845 leads northwards to the busy **fishing port** of Húsavík. Situated on an attractive harbour and backed by snow-capped mountains, Húsavík has a population of around 2500 and is the main service centre for northeast Iceland.

THE GODAR AND THE FALLS

Way back in the year 1000, the 'goðar', or pagan chieftains, had a heated debate at the **Althing** about whether to abandon pagan-ism and adopt Christianity. The decision was finally left to the **law-speaker**, Thorgeir Thorkelsson. He is said to have curled up under his sheepskin in a booth at Thingvellir for three days and nights while he considered the problem. He finally came up with a classic compromise, deciding in favour of Christianity, but allowing the people to practice paganism in the privacy of their homes if they so wished. To set a good example, Thorgeir, on his way home, threw his pagan effigies into the water-falls – thereafter to be known as the 'Waterfall of the Gods', or **Goðafoss**.

Above: *Húsavík's distinctive church, built with timber brought from Norway.*

Húsavík's first inhabitant was a Viking named Garðar Svavarsson. He gave up and left after the first winter, but two of his slaves were unfortunately left behind. In reality these were Iceland's very first settlers, but they are never credited as such. Today Húsavík makes its living mainly from fish processing, sulphur exports and tourism. In recent years the town has become Iceland's most important **whale-watching centre**. Over 90 per cent of trips record minke whales, while other cetaceans commonly seen are humpbacks, fins, sei and orcas, plus harbour porpoises and dolphins. A **Whale Museum** is currently being developed. The town museum, the **Safnahúsið**, is also worth a visit. As well as the usual social memorabilia, there is also a stuffed polar bear, which was washed up on the island of Grímsey and greeted with a bullet.

There are two islands in Skjálfandi Bay, namely **Flatey** and **Lundey**, which are easily reached by boat from Húsavík. The latter is particularly noted for its large colony of puffins.

GRÍMSEY

Some 41km (25 miles) north of the mainland is the island of Grímsey. Covering an area of 5.3km² (2 sq miles), it straddles the Arctic Circle (visitors can obtain documents certifying that they have crossed over into the Arctic). Only 120 people live on the island, mainly around the harbour at Sandvík. Ferries and planes connect it to Grímsey, especially in the summer months. Most visitors are bird-watchers. The cliffs teem with sea birds during the breeding season, with guillemots, puffins, razorbills, fulmars and even a few pairs of the rare little auk.

GRÍMSEY'S AMERICAN BENEFACTOR

One of the most remarkable stories of 19th-century Iceland was the strange tale of an American millionaire named **Daniel Willard Fiske**, who befriended the people of Grímsey, largely, it seems, because of their enthusiasm for playing chess. Although he never set foot on the island, he poured in resources such as money and firewood. He also arranged for a school and a library to be built. Fiske, who was the American **chess champion**, sent over 11 marble chess sets – one for each farm on the island. Ironically, few people on Grímsey are interested in the game today.

LAKE MÝVATN AREA

This is one of the most important tourist locations in Iceland, currently receiving an estimated 100,000 visitors a year. Apart from the lake itself, which attracts bird-watchers from all over the world, there are a host of volcanic features to observe. The climate, too, is agreeable as the area is in the rain shadow of the Vatnajökull icecap, making it one of the driest parts of the country.

Lake Mývatn ***

The lake, which sits on the Mid-Atlantic Ridge, covers around 37km² (14 sq miles). It is essentially a shallow lake, with an average depth of 2.5m (8.2ft). This means that light can penetrate right to the bottom, making it rich in vegetation and nutrients, which in turn prove attractive to wildfowl. The numbers of ducks present in the summer are staggering, with probably around 50,000 pairs and 15 species represented. These include tufted duck, wigeon, mergansers, long-tailed duck, teal, gadwall and goosanders. Add to this list whooper swans, slavonian grebe, red-necked phalarope, skuas, terns, snow buntings and snowy owl, and it is clear why birders flock here in huge numbers. European bird-watchers in particular are keen to see American species such as Barrow's goldeneye and harlequin duck (which breeds along the River Laxa).

A metalled road runs along the east of the lake and a dirt track follows the western side. A large area in the northwest of the lake is a protected nesting area and out of bounds for much of the summer. Although much of

PSEUDO CRATERS

A feature of the Mývatn area is the large number of **islands** in the lake (about 50) and the numerous small hills in the vicinity. On inspection they are seen to have concave summits and are described by geologists as **pseudo craters**, largely because no lava ever flowed out of them. They were formed when lava flowed across the lake. The trapped water boiled and exploded through the lava, building up cones and craters. They vary in size from 250m (820ft) to 3m (9ft) across.

Below: *The shallow waters of Lake Mývatn teem with a variety of wildfowl.*

Mývatn ices over in winter, part of the northern section is fed by hot springs and remains ice-free, so that there are wildfowl present throughout the year. Bird-watchers and other visitors should beware of insects. Mývatn means 'lake of the midges' and there are swarms of these little pests, especially on calm days in the summer. Net head covers are recommended.

The lake contains over 50 islands, most of which are **pseudo craters**. They look like mini volcanoes, but were in fact formed by gas explosions. This gives a hint of the **volcanic features** which abound in the area, particularly to the northeast of the lake. There has been continual volcanic activity since the end of the Ice Age. Particularly significant were the '**Mývatn fires**' which flowed from the Krafla area between 1724 and 1729 along a fissure which is still occasionally active. More recent were the '**Krafla fires**' in the early 1980s. Subterranean rumblings suggest that more volcanic activity is imminent. Many of the volcanic features can be viewed at first hand.

Dimmuborgir **

Dimmuborgir, which can be translated as 'black castles', is an area of lava located on the eastern side of the lake.

Lake Mývatn

Thought to be around 2000 years old, the lava here is believed to have been dammed by older material and then forced up into a wide variety of contorted shapes. It is possible for visitors to wander around among the lava pillars, caves and holes, which are now developing some interesting vegetation. To save the area from human erosion, set walking routes have been roped off – but it is still quite possible for people to get lost!

Hverfjall *

Just north of Dimmuborgir stands the cinder cone of Hverfjall which rises to 163m (534ft). It was formed during a cataclysmic eruption around 2500 years ago. It is possible to walk up the steep path to the rim of the crater, though hikers are no longer allowed to descend to the crater floor.

Above: *The Viti explosion crater and lake situated on the slopes of the frequently active Krafla.*

Hot Springs *

Situated between Hverfjall and the village of Reykjahíð are a couple of popular hot springs which give visitors an opportunity for bathing. The first, **Stóragjá**, is hidden in a crevice and has to be reached by means of a rope ladder, but the second, **Grjótagjá**, is much more accessible and is divided into separate sections for men and women. The water temperatures are generally around 47°C (116°F), but are cooling annually.

Krafla ***

To the northeast of the lake is the impressive Krafla volcanic complex. It is readily accessible, with visitors able to drive there directly from the Ring Road, passing the Krafla Geothermal Power Station en route. Krafla itself does not resemble the archetypal cone-shaped volcano, but is in fact a reasonably level system of fissures, along which the surface occasionally swells and erupts. Nearby, however, is the dramatic **Viti explosion crater**. Viti is the Icelandic name for 'hell' and the 320m (1049ft) wide crater, which often fills with ice floes in the winter, certainly fits the description.

Hverarönd ***

About 6km (3.7 miles) to the east of the lake, at the side of the Ring Road and situated on the Mid-Atlantic Ridge, is the hill known as **Námafjall**. Among its cracks and fissures are bands of yellow sulphur. The mineral was

---

COPING WITH THE MIDGES

One of the less appealing aspects of Lake Mývatn is the swarms of midges which gave the lake its name. They hatch between June and August and can make life very unpleasant. They seem particularly attracted to the **carbon dioxide** on people's breath and seem intent on entering the nose, eyes, ears and mouth. They are particularly active on **calm days** and reduce in number the further you are from the lake. Insect repellent and net headware are strongly recommended. The good news is that the midges do not bite (although the blackfly certainly does – it can be readily identified by its buzzing noise). Midges are eagerly devoured by wildfowl and fish. In fact, the Laxa River is reputed to have the country's biggest salmon as a result of this.

Above: *Part of the lava flow that threatened the church at Reykjalíð in 1929.*
Opposite: *Dettifoss is claimed to be Europe's most powerful waterfall in terms of water volume.*

DIATOMS

The bed of Lake Mývatn has a layer of diatomaceous ooze which is up to 15m (49ft) thick. Diatomite is the skeletal remains of diatoms, which are microscopic single-cell **algae**. The fossil shells are one ten-thousandth the size of a grain of sand and consist largely of silica. The diatomite is sucked up from a barge and pumped by pipeline to the processing plant, where it is dried using steam from the nearby Bjarnaflag geothermal power station. The result is a white powder which is packed and transported to Húsavík, from whence it is **exported** to Europe for use as a filler in a variety of industries.

---

once mined here, but was not commercially successful. Beneath the hill is the remarkable area of **Hverarönd**, undoubtly one of Iceland's most unforgettable sights. There are bubbling mud pools, steam vents, hot boiling springs, fumeroles and the distinctive stench of sulphur everywhere. Visitors are advised to stick to the roped-off paths as some of the surface material is fragile.

Reykjahlíð ★★★

This is the only settlement of any size in the Mývatn area. Though originally merely a farmhouse, it has grown in size with the development of tourism and is now an important service centre for the surrounding region. There is a church, hotel, supermarket, tourist office, bank and small museum. The original church was threatened by the 1929 lava flow which completely destroyed many of the buildings in the village, but miraculously the flow passed by a few metres from the church. A modern church was built on the site in 1972 and is well worth a visit.

The Reykjahlíð area has seen a number of industrial ventures, some of which have been successful, others spectacular failures. The main employer at the moment is the Bjarnaflag **diatomite plant**, which is fortunately well away from the lake. Diatoms are microfossils which are dredged up from the lake bed. After treatment they are used as a filler in such products as paint and toothpaste. The diatomaceous ooze is moved by pipeline to the refining plant just north of the Ring Road. There are environmental questions about the effect the dredging is having on the ecology of the lake, and naturalists are particularly worried about operations moving to other parts of the lake. Though diatomite mining is highly successful, the **Krafla Geothermal Power Station** has been a dubious operation and its drilling is believed to have set off the Krafla eruptions in the mid-70s. Before leaving the area, take a look at the land on the opposite side of the road to the diatom plant. This is marked by a pipe with steam bursting out of it and was the site of a drill hole to ascertain the feasibility of locating a geothermal power station here. Just by its side is an underground bread oven. Peer through the glass doors to see the *hverabrauð* taking 24 hours to bake.

JÖKULSÁRGLJÚFUR NATIONAL PARK ★★★

Jökulsárgljúfur was given its national park status in 1978. It is essentially a 30km (18.5-mile) canyon formed by *jökulhlaup*, or glacial meltwater floods. The canyon is drained by the River **Jökulsá á Fjöllum**, which rises on the Vatnjökull icecap and then flows north for 206km (127 miles) to the Arctic Ocean. Jökulsárgljúfur is often described as 'Iceland's Grand Canyon' and although its measurements cannot compare with the American giant, it is certainly an impressive sight. The main part of the canyon averages 100m (330ft) in depth and has a width of 500m (547yd). There is a series of impressive waterfalls, including Hafragilsfoss, Dettifoss and Selfoss. Of these, **Dettifoss** should not be missed, as it is claimed to be Europe's most powerful waterfall. Although only 45m (150ft) in height, it dispatches some 500m³ (17,657ft³) of water per second – a truly awesome sight. Downstream from here is another extraordinary landform, detached from the main canyon and known as **Ásbyrgi**. It is a dry, horseshoe-shaped gorge, which the Vikings believed was the hoofprint of Odin's horse. The geographical explanation is that it is an incised abandoned meander, left high and dry when the Jökulsá á Fjöllum changed its course during a *jökulhlaup*. Fulmars breed on the walls of the gorge in summer. The national park is wonderful for hiking, but there is no formal accommodation within the park, and just two official campsites. The national park brochure indicates the main walking trails.

THE SNOWY OWL

Few sights are more evocative of Iceland than the flight of the white, ghostly snowy owl. This magnificent bird is **diurnal** and largely solitary. It can often be seen sitting upright on a low eminence, surveying the surrounding land for prey. It is resident in Iceland, but has become **extremely rare**, being largely confined to the more inaccessible areas – although some have been seen in the Mývatn area in recent years. Snowy owls usually prey on ptarmigan, but will take young ducks and goslings in the breeding season.

Northern Iceland at a Glance

BEST TIMES TO VISIT

As with most parts of the country, the summer months from June to September are the most convenient times to visit the north of Iceland. At this period the area is drier than it is in the south, and it also has more sunny days. At this northerly latitude there is scarcely any night at all during the summer. The winter months are not recommended for visitors, due to the heavy snowfall, the cold blasts of wind from the Arctic, and the lack of daylight, particularly during the months of December, January and February.

GETTING THERE

The Ring Road is usually kept open during winter, but may be temporarily closed from time to time during heavy snowfalls until the snow can be cleared from the surface. Akureyri is approximately 390km (242 miles) by road from Reykjavík. BSÍ coaches take the better part of a day to cover this distance. It is much quicker to reach the northern parts of the country by air. The airline **Flugleiðir** operates daily flights from Reykjavík to Akureyri, and less regular flights to Grimsey, Húsavík and Sauðárkrókur. Another local airline, **Flugfélag Norðurlands**, which is based in Akureyri, has daily incoming flights from Reykjavík.

GETTING AROUND

The Ring Road is very well surfaced throughout the north of Iceland, and cars have no problems during summer. However, 4WD vehicles are generally recommended for travelling here in winter. The main settlements in the area are all linked by bus, but away from the Ring Road bus services may be confined to one or two services a day. Cars and 4WD vehicles may be hired in Akureyri and in Sauðárkrókur.

WHERE TO STAY

There is no accommodation in the international luxury range in northern Iceland. There are, however, several comfortable hotels in the mid-range.

MID-RANGE

Hotel KEA, Hafnarstræti 87–89, 600 Akureyri, tel: 460 2000, fax: 460 2060, e-mail: kea@keahotel.is Situated in the shadow of the church, this hotel has all the facilities, but on a busy road.
Hotel Reynihlíð, 660 Reykjahlíð, Mývatn, tel: 464 4710, fax: 464 4371. The accommodation price includes a continental buffet breakfast.
The Edda Group runs a number of hotels in the area, some are summer hotels. They are found at Laugarbakka, Blönduós and Akureyri. E-mail: edda@icehotel.is
The Foss Group have hotels at Laugar, Fosshóll, near Goðafoss, Sauðárkrókur and two in Akureyri. Some are summer hotels. E-mail: bokun@fosshotel.is
Hotel Odal, Hafnarstræti 67, Akureyri, tel: 461 1900, fax: 461 1899. Recently-built hotel near the harbour.
Hotel Varmahlíð, 560 Varmahlíð, tel: 453 8170, fax: 453 8870. Modern hotel right on the Ring Road. Best restaurant in the area.

BUDGET

Akureyri Guesthouse, Strandgata 23, Akureyri, tel: 462 2720, fax: 462 7240. Basic, good value rooms on pedestrianized street.
Árból Guesthouse, Asgarðsvegur 2, 640 Húsavik, tel: 464 2220. Plain bedrooms and shared bathrooms. Friendly owners. Open all year.
Gistiheimilið Hraunbrún, Reykjahlíð, tel: 464 4103. This is a good centre for the Mývatn area. Next to the campground.
Gistiheimilið Ás, Skipagata 4, 600 Akureyri, tel: 461 2248, fax: 461 3810. Centrally located near bus station. Some self-catering units are available.
Youth Hostels can be found at Akureyri, at Ósar (near Hvammstangi in the west of the region), and at Sæberg, near Brú. For booking, tel: 533 8110, fax: 588 9201.
Campsites: two in the Jökulsá National Park, three at Mývatn, and others at Akureyri, Blönduós, Goðafoss, Sauðár-krókur and Ólafsfjörður. These are all official seasonal sites.

Northern Iceland at a Glance

WHERE TO EAT

The best restaurants in the north of the country are invariably those in hotel dining rooms, and in the more remote areas these are often the only option in the evenings. Hotel restaurants, however, are usually rather expensive. There are a few other restaurants in the larger settlements which can be recommended:

Sauðárkrókur
MID-RANGE
Kaffi Krókur, Aðalgata 16, Sauðárkrókur, tel: 453 6299. This is a cosy restaurant in the heart of the town, serving Icelandic food in a cosmopolitan setting.

Akureyri
MID-RANGE
Bautinn, Hafnarstræti 92, tel: 462 1818. Here mountains of food are to be had at bargain prices, served in an atrium-like setting.
Greifinn, Glerágata 20, tel: 461 2690. This restaurant serves moderately priced Icelandic food as well as a selection of burgers, pizzas and pasta.

Mývatn
MID-RANGE
Gamli Bærinn, Reykjalið, tel: 464 4170. This restaurant serves an excellent meal of the day packed with local specialities, including the cake-like *hverabrauð*.

Húsavík
MID-RANGE
Gamli Baukur, tel: 464 2442. Well-cooked fresh fish in a popular wooden harbourside restaurant.

BUDGET
Cheaper options are found at **snack bars** attached to service stations, which usually have a filling tourist menu.

TOURS AND EXCURSIONS

Many tours and excursions around the popular venues in the north can be booked in Reykjavík, but a number of local firms can arrange tours for small groups, particularly for adventure trips.
Hestasport, located at the Vindheimamelar racing grounds 20km (12 miles) south of Varmalið, Raftahlíð 20, 550 Sauðárkrókur, tel: 453 5066. Arranges riding tours as well as trips to experience the autumn *rettir* (sheep round-ups).
Activity Tours, tel: 453 5066. This firm specializes in whitewater rafting trips.
Nonni Travel, Ráðhúsplads, Akureyri, tel: 461 1841, arranges excursions to Hólar and Grimsey by ferry and by

air. This company also offers excursions in the Mývatn area amongst many others. For whale-watching tours from Húsavík, contact **North Sailing**, on the harbourside, tel: 464 2350. They use traditional Icelandic oak boats. Alternatively try **Sjóferðir-Arnar**, also located on the harbourside, tel: 464 1748.

USEFUL CONTACTS

Tourist Information Centres are situated at all the major settlements in the north. The most important one is in **Akureyri** at the bus terminal, Hafnarstræti 82, tel: 462 7733. It is open from June–August, weekdays from 09:00–21:00, weekends from 12:00–20:00. Also from September–May, weekdays from 08:30–17:00.
Other Tourist Information Centres can be found at:
Blönduós, situated at the campground, tel: 452 4520;
Varmahlið, at the Shell petrol station, tel: 453 8860;
Sauðárkrókur, at the Fosshotel Áning, tel: 453 6717;
Mývatn, at Reykjahliðar school, tel: 464 4390; and
Húsavík, Ketilsbraut 22, tel: 464 2520.

AKUREYRI	J	F	M	A	M	J	J	A	S	O	N	D
AVE. TEMP. °C	-2.2	-2.6	-2.6	0.7	7.2	9.9	12.5	10.5	6.3	3.7	1.7	-0.5
AVE. TEMP. °F	28	27.3	27.3	33.3	44.9	49.8	54.5	50.9	43.3	38.6	35	31.1
AVE. RAINFALL mm	55.2	42.5	43.3	29.2	19.3	28.2	33	34.1	39.1	58	54.2	52.8
AVE. RAINFALL in	2.17	1.67	1.7	1.15	0.76	1.11	1.3	1.34	1.54	2.29	2.14	2.08

6
East Iceland

Remote from the Mid-Atlantic Ridge, East Iceland is the country's geologically most stable and oldest area. It consists largely of basalt, a rock which flowed large distances from long-lost volcanoes. The whole area was later **glaciated**. Moving down from corries high in the mountains, the glaciers gouged out deep, U-shaped valleys, which were later flooded – in the post-glacial rise in sea level – to form today's impressive **fiords**. The Ring Road from Mývatn in the north to Egilsstaðir passes through one of Iceland's most majestic features: a **cold desert**, which is almost completely devoid of vegetation. The southwest boundary of the region is marked by the edge of **Vatnajökull**, Europe's largest icecap, from which numerous **glaciers** run down to the coastal plain.

The main service and transportation centre for the area is the rather unremarkable town of **Egilsstaðir**, which is located in the **Largafljót Valley**. The river here flows through **Lake Lögurinn**, which is 100m (330ft) deep. It is also Iceland's longest lake and reputedly has a resident monster. The slopes of the valley are clothed with the country's largest and most mature forest, which has a network of footpaths for exploring the woods. Each fiord has a small fishing port, the most important of these being **Seyðisfjörður**, **Djúpivogur** and **Reyðar-fjörður**. Further to the south is the sheltered port and communications centre of **Höfn**, the first major settlement on the Ring Road since Selfoss, approximately 400km (250 miles) away to the west.

DON'T MISS

*** The Cold Desert: the fascinating mountain desert in the rain shadow of the Vatnajökull icecap.
** The Eastern Fiords: a region of fishing villages and lovely Scandinavian-style wooden buildings.
** Lake Lögurinn: a deep ribbon lake, reputedly with its own resident monster.
** Petra's Rock Museum: Petra Sveinsdóttir's private collection of rocks, minerals and fossils, displayed in her house and garden.

Opposite: *The ptarmigan, Iceland's most common game bird. Many are taken annually by gyrfalcons.*

CLIMATE

It is claimed that the Eastern Fiords have Iceland's most agreeable climate. Sitting in the rain shadow of the Vatnajökull icecap, the **rainfall** is low by Icelandic standards. **Summers** are sunny and mild. **Winters** can be wet, but snow is only heavy on the mountains, and the area is protected from cold Arctic winds.

PTARMIGAN

The ptarmigan is Iceland's only game bird and is seen throughout the highland areas of the country. It is essentially a bird of the tundra and feeds mainly on the shoots of heather, crowberry and bilberry. The ptarmigan has the ability to moult three times a year to adapt to changing environmental conditions, so that it may be pure white in the winter snows, but a patterned grey-brown during the summer. Camouflage is the ptarmigan's main form of defence, and the female sitting on eggs is almost impossible to spot. Its main predator is the gyrfalcon, which can reduce the ptarmigan's numbers by as much as a third in a season.

Seyðisfjörður is Iceland's only car ferry link with Europe. From the ferry port, drivers once had to take the northerly route to Reykjavík via Mývatn, but in 1974 the Ring Road was completed. This allowed cars to take the southerly option, cutting both time and distance considerably. Few motorists stop for long in the eastern fiords region, with the result that it has none of the usual trappings of tourism, thus adding to its attractions for the discriminating visitor.

CROSSING THE DESERT

The route between Mývatn and Egilsstaðir crosses an interior cold desert which is one of the most fascinating parts of the country. The Ring Road, which is largely surfaced by gravel in this region, passes bare plains covered with volcanic ash and the glacial deposits of occasional meltwater floods. It climbs remote rocky passes and bridges rushing streams, with hardly a single item of vegetation to be seen. On a fine day, the journey is full of interest, but in the mist and rain, it can have a brooding, rather sinister atmosphere. Surprisingly there are two small isolated areas of farming here. At the northern end of the road, close to the Jökulsá á Fjöllum River,

Right: *The tiny church at Möðrudalur, built by a local farmer in memory of his wife.*

is the remote farm of **Grímsstaðir**. The road here was once crossed by ferry, and the old ferryman's hut, reputed to be haunted, can still be seen in the distance. Further south is the little oasis of **Möðrudalur**. At 469m (1358ft), this is almost certainly the highest farm in the country. Buses stop here for half an hour or so, to allow passengers to use the snack bar and toilets. It is worth strolling over the road to see a small church, built by the local farmer in 1949 in memory of his wife. Note its unconventional altarpiece. This particular stretch of the Ring Road gives excellent views of **Herðubreið** (the name means 'broad-shouldered'), a plateau-like mountain capped with a volcanic cone. Composed of palagonite, it rises to a height of 1060m (3500ft) and dominates the surrounding area. The Ring Road then crosses a high pass capped with cairns, which are said to mark the boundary of the bishoprics of Hólar and Skálholt, before dropping down into the valley of the **Jökulsa á Dal**.

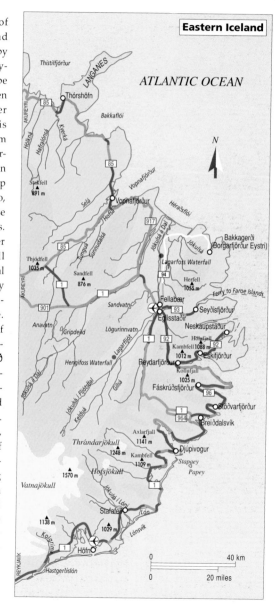

Eastern Iceland

ATLANTIC OCEAN

Above: *East Iceland is the most likely part of the country to spot small herds of wild reindeer.*

EGILSSTAÐIR

Originally just a farmstead on the eastern bank of the Lagarfljót river, Egilsstaðir has grown rapidly with the completion of the Ring Road and the development of air travel, so that it is now the transportation and service centre for the whole of eastern Iceland. It has a population of around 1600 and, despite its rather sterile look, it makes a good centre for exploring the surrounding area. There is little to see in the town itself, apart from the modern geological theme **church** and a **folk museum** which also includes a restored farmhouse. The River Lagafljót, which is about 140km (86 miles) long, is Iceland's second longest river. Its murky glacial flood-waters are crossed by one of the country's longest bridges, some 310m (339yd) in length, which links Egilsstaðir with the altogether more attractive village of **Fellabær** on the western bank.

Around Egilsstaðir ★★★

To the north of the town, Route 94 leads to the bay of **Héraðsflói**, where the Jökulsá á Dal and Lagaflót rivers form a delta, with marshes and coastal sand dunes. At the farmstead of **Húsey** there is a youth hostel. This is an excellent bird-watching area, particularly for waders and geese.

South of Egilsstaðir, the river flows through **Lake Lögurinn**. This long, deep ribbon lake is reputed to have a resident monster. The eastern shores of the lake are clothed with some of Iceland's most mature trees, one rising to the princely height of 15m (50ft)! This is excellent walking country, with its many hiking trails and picnic sites. Further trails to the south of the lake lead to

---

THE MONSTER OF THE DEEP

Many of the deep glaciated ribbon lakes of the world, probably not coincidentally, have stories of resident monsters. Despite state-of-the-art, high technology research at many sites, nowhere has the presence of a 'monster' been conclusively proven. Lake Lögurinn, to the south of Egilsstaðir, is no exception. Despite centuries of rumours of the existence of a dragon-like creature, there is no hard evidence available. Nevertheless, in a country in which a survey of over 50 per cent of the population showed a lack of denial over the existence of elves, anything is possible!

the waterfalls of **Hengifoss** (Iceland's third highest) and **Lagarfoss**, the latter of which has a small power plant and a fish ladder for migrating salmon. A further track, accessible by four-wheel-drive vehicles, leads to a boggy moorland and the extinct volcano of **Snæfell**. At 1833m (6013ft), it is the highest mountain in the country outside the icecaps. It is also as good a place as any in Iceland for seeing wild reindeer.

THE EASTERN FIORDS

Though lacking the rugged grandeur of their counterparts in the northwest of Iceland, the Eastern Fiords are scenically one of the most pleasant areas of the country. The fiords are generally aligned east–west, so that the settlements are usually on the north (south-facing) sides of the water, to receive the maximum benefit of the sun. There is a string of small fishing ports, which gained considerable prosperity in the days of the herring boom, so that their wooden houses have a wealthy Scandinavian feel about them. Despite having a reputation for the best weather in Iceland, few tourists stay in this area for long. Those that do stay have the benefit of missing the crowds.

> ### REFORESTATION
>
> On the eastern bank of Lake Lögurinn lies the **Hallormsstaðarskógur**, Iceland's largest area of forest. Over 50 varieties of trees are seen here, mainly types of conifer, birch and poplar. This has been the headquarters of the **State Forestry Service** since 1907. They have searched the world for species which will survive in Iceland's harsh climate. It is quite probable that Iceland was covered with trees in the days of the Viking settlement, but that they were quickly removed for fuel and building material, and regeneration was prevented by sheep grazing. Today, there are a number of organizations throughout the country, in both rural and urban areas, engaged in planting trees, using the advice of the State Forestry Service.

Left: *Trees on the State Forestry Service's land on the eastern bank of Lake Lögurinn, near Egilsstaðir.*

Borgarfjörður Eystri ***

Due north of Egilsstaðir, and reached by way of Route 94 and the stunning mountain range of **Dyrfjöll**, is the small village of Borgarfjörður Eystri (shown on some maps as Bakkagerði). This was the home of Iceland's best-known landscape artist, **Jóhannes S Karvel**. The village church has an altarpiece painted by Karvel, representing the Sermon on the Mount.

Seyðisfjörður *

Due east of Egilsstaðir and connected by Route 93 is the **ferry port** of Seyðisfjörður. For many people this will be their first glimpse of Iceland – and they are rarely disappointed. It sits at the head of a narrow curving fiord backed by snow-capped mountains. The attractive harbourside buildings are made of wood, all mainly constructed by a Norwegian entrepreneur in the middle of the 19th century, when it was an important trading port. The *Norræna* ferry runs a scheduled service in the summer, connecting Seyðisfjörður with the Faroe Islands, Shetland, Norway and Denmark.

Neskaupstaður *

The next settlement is Neskaupstaður which, with a population of over 1600, is the **largest town** in East Iceland. Owing to its remote position, it is bypassed by most tourists. In fact, it was not linked to the rest of the country by road until 1947. Today, its economy is largely involved in fish-related industries. Just to the southwest is the fishing and trading port of **Eskifjörður**, backed by the attractive mountain Hólmatindur which rises to some 985m (3231 ft). The town is mainly noted for its **Maritime Museum**.

Below: *The garden of Petra's Stone Museum at Stöðvarfjörður.*

Housed in a 19th-century warehouse, it is filled with fishing and whaling artefacts. In the hills behind the town is an old Iceland Spar mine which, although it is now closed down, was once the world's biggest producer of this mineral.

Reyðarfjörður ***

This town is located at the head of the fiord of the same name, in the midst of rich farmland. Reyðarfjörður was an important Allied base during World War II, and a **Museum of War Memorabilia** opened here in 1995. The Ring Road reaches the coast near Breiðalsvík. Reyðarfjörður is the site of a controversial aluminium smelting works due to open in 2005. It is worth visiting the small fishing village of **Stöðvarfjörður** just to see the amazing **Rock Museum**. Situated in a private house, it is the personal collection of Petra Sveinsdóttir. Rocks, fossils and minerals seem to fill every corner, along with the odd stuffed bird and ancient household artefact.

Djúpivogur *

Of the remaining fishing villages, only Djúpivogur is of interest. It is located on a headland on the southern side of Berufjörður and backed by the pyramid-shaped Búlandstindur, which rises to 1090m (3575ft). Djúpivogur was an important **Danish trading station** as far back as the 16th century, and some of the oldest houses in the town today were built by Danish merchants. The *Löngubúð* warehouse on the harbourside has been restored and is now the **local museum and art gallery**. Just offshore is the island of **Papey**, which was once a hermitage for Irish monks, until they fled at the arrival of the Norsemen. Today the island is uninhabited, apart from its seals and sea birds. Cruises run from Djúpivogur to Papey during the summer months.

Above: *The harbour at Djúpivogur. An old warehouse in the port has been converted into an interesting folk museum.*

THE YULETIDE LADS

As Christmas approaches, Iceland's version of Santa Claus puts in an appearance. These are the **Yuletide Lads**, or *jólasveinar*. In the country's folklore they were child-eating ogres who descended from the mountains in groups of 13, in homespun clothes, to play pranks on people. Nowadays, influenced by the commercial Father Christmas image from other parts of the world, the Yuletide Lads have adopted the red garments and long white beards of the traditional Santa Claus. An Icelandic horse, however, is more likely to pull their sledge than a red-nosed reindeer.

Above: *Numerous glacier tongues run down from the Vatnajökull icecap.*

A HIGHLY PRIZED FALCON

Europe's largest falcon is the magnificent **gyrfalcon**, and Iceland is one of its strongholds. Specially pro-tected, around 200 pairs remain, scattered around the country wherever its main prey, the ptarmigan, is found. For many centuries, the gyrfalcon was one of Iceland's most valuable exports, as it was highly prized for falconry and hunting. It is estimated that during the Middle Ages over 200 birds were exported annually. Falconry still exists in many countries in the world and there is an illicit smuggling trade in gyrfalcon chicks and eggs. Gyrfalcons usually nest on cliff ledges, often in an old raven's nest, if necessary evicting the ravens first.

Höfn ***

The Ring Road skirts the first of the *sandur* which mark the southern side of the Vatnajökull icecap. The main town and **port** of this stretch of the coast is Höfn. The name means 'harbour', and its pronunciation can best be described as a 'hiccup'. It is located on Hornafjörður, which is in fact a bay that is almost completely enclosed by two spits, the narrow entrance calling for skilful navigation.

The completion of the Ring Road has boosted Höfn's **population**, which is fast approaching 2000. Fishing, farming and tourism are the main sources of employment.

The **Regional Folk Museum** in the town is worth a look. Based in an old warehouse, it has displays on local fishing, farming and wildlife. Open 10:00–12:00 and 14:00–17:00, June–August.

Don't miss the **Glacier Exhibition** in Hafnabraut. Full of information about glacial action and jökulhlaups, including a 10-minute video on glaciers and volcanoes .

Höfn is also the main centre for arranging tours to the **Vatnasárlón icecap** and to the **Jökulsárlón Glacial Lagoon** (*see* chapter 7 for information on both). There are icecap tours available by snowmobile, and also by glacier buggy, skiddoo and by ski. However, visitors are warned not to venture out on to the icecap independent-ly, but to use the expert guides that are available and take their advice regarding equipment and clothing.

East Iceland at a Glance

BEST TIMES TO VISIT

The summer, June–August, is the best time, particularly if arriving by car ferry from the Faroes, Scandinavia and Scotland. The eastern fiords have the most favourable climate and here visiting season can be extended into May and September.

GETTING THERE

This is the only part of Iceland that can be approached by **ship** from abroad. The ferry *Norröna*, run by the Faeroese Smyril Line, operates a weekly service in summer, linking Seyðisfjörður with Esbjerg in Denmark, Bergen in Norway, Tórshavn in the Faroe Islands, and Shetland. The **road** route to the area is via the Ring Road; the southern route is quicker and shorter than the northern route. Bus services connect the main towns on the Ring Road. Flugleiðir and Flugfélag have **air** services from Egilsstaðir to Höfn, Akureyri and Reykjavík.

GETTING AROUND

Apart from a private car, the only option for getting around the region is by bus. There are services daily around the Ring Road, but routes linking the fiord ports are less regular. Be prepared for a reduced timetable in winter.

WHERE TO STAY

There are no hotels in the luxury range, but plenty of choice in the other categories.

MID-RANGE

Hotel Höfn, 780 Horna-fjörður, tel: 478 1240, fax: 478 1996, e-mail: hofn@icehotel.is Also has a cheaper annexe.
Hotel Snæfell, Austarvegur 3, 710 Seyðisfjörður, tel: 472 1460, fax: 472 1570. Harbour-side hotel convenient for ferry.
Hotel Egilsbuð, Egilsbraut 1, Neskaupstaður, tel: 477 1321, fax: 477 1322. Near harbour.
Hotel Framtíð, Vogaland 4, 765 Djúpivogur, tel: 478 8887, fax: 478 8187, e-mail framtid@simnet.is Overlooks the harbour; good restaurant. The **Edda Group** has hotels at Egilsstaðir, Hallormsstaður and Höfn, and the **Foss Group** at Vatnajökull and Hallormsstaður. Some are summer hotels. For booking: Edda, tel: 505 0910; Foss, tel: 471 1705.

BUDGET

Guesthouse Skipalækur, Fellabær, tel: 471 1324. Sleeping bag accommodation and some lakeside chalets.
Youth Hostels at Höfn, Reyðarfjörður and Seyðis-fjörður. Booking, tel: 553 8110.
Campsites at Borgafjörður, Egilsstaðir, Neskaupstaður, Eskifjörður, Reydarfjörður, Breiðdalsvík and Höfn.

WHERE TO EAT

Good restaurants are scarce outside hotel dining rooms, but most service station snack bars serve a good tourist menu.

BUDGET

Ormurinn, Kaupvangur 2, Egilsstaðir, tel: 471 2321. Chicken and pasta dishes.

TOURS AND EXCURSIONS

In Egilsstaðir, **Austurlands Travel**, tel: 471 2000, and **Lagarfljötsormurinn**, tel: 471 2900, offer boat trips on Lake Lörgurinn, while **Tanni Travel**, tel: 476 1399, arranges hikes around the Snæfell area and buggy trips on Vatnajökull. **Papeyjarferðir**, tel: 478 8183, runs cruises in summer from Djúpivogur to the island of Papey. In Höfn, **Glacier Tours**, tel: 478 1000, run snowmobile and jeep tours on and around Vatnajökull.

USEFUL CONTACTS

Major **Tourist Information Centres** are at Egilsstaðir, tel: 471 2320; at Seyðisfjörður (in the Smyril Line building), tel: 472 1111; and at Höfn (a private TIC at the camp-ground), tel: 478 1701.

EGILSSTAÐIR	J	F	M	A	M	J	J	A	S	O	N	D
AVE. TEMP. °C	0.3	0.6	0.1	1.4	3.3	6.2	8	8.3	6.6	4.5	1.8	0.6
AVE. TEMP. °F	32.5	33	32.2	34.5	37.9	43.2	46.4	46.9	43.9	40.1	35.2	33
AVE. RAINFALL mm	134	103	116	87	93	87	97	114	180	169	129	121
AVE. RAINFALL in	5.28	4.05	4.57	3.42	3.66	3.42	3.82	4.49	7.09	6.66	5.08	4.77

7
South Iceland

The central part of South Iceland is dominated by the huge mass of the **Vatnajökull icecap**, which is Europe's largest ice sheet and the third largest in the world. Iceland's highest mountain, **Hvannadalshnjúkur** at 2119m (6950ft), pokes its head above the ice. **Glaciers** snake their way down from the icecap, most prominently in a southerly direction. Lurking under the ice are several **volcanoes**, such as **Grimsvötn**, which periodically erupt and melt large quantities of ice, causing glacial floods or *jökulhlaups*. As well as causing widespread damage, these *jökulhlaups* have built up huge spreads of sand and gravel known as *sandur*. It was these *sandur* which prevented the completion of the Ring Road until 1974. Only after this date was the south central part of Iceland opened up for tourism.

Just to the southwest of Vatnajökull is a smaller icecap, **Mýrdalsjökull**, which also has a subglacial volcano, **Katla**. Here, again, there is a *sandur* to the south. The area around the icecaps has a wealth of places for tourists to visit and few fail to be impressed with **Jökulsárlón**, a glacial lagoon where calving icebergs can be viewed from a boat. **Skaftafell**, Iceland's largest national park and the second to be proclaimed, is also popular with visitors and offers good hiking possibilities amongst stunning scenery. Snowmobile and ice-buggy trips on the two icecaps are another favourite tourist activity. Waterfalls abound, including the impressive **Svartifoss** (named after its black lava columns) and **Skógafoss**. There are several places of interest for bird-watchers. The *sandur*

DON'T MISS

*** The Icecaps:** try a snow-mobile or glacier buggy ride on Vatnajökull or Mydalsjökull.
*** Jökulsárlón Lagoon:** take a boat trip among the icebergs and seals.
*** The Interior:** cross the wild and uninhabited interior by 4WD vehicle.
*** Skaftafell National Park:** attractive area with a variety of scenery and wildlife.
** The Coast around Vík:** cliffs, stacks and beaches, full of breeding sea birds.
** The *Sandur*:** huge sand and gravel plains deposited by glacial floods.

Opposite: *Skógafoss, one of Iceland's highest waterfalls, drops into a narrow gorge.*

Above: *Svínafellsjökull, an accessible glacial tongue in Skaftafell National Park.*

contain Iceland's largest concentration of skuas, while the cliffs and stacks at **Dyrhólaey** have a good selection of breeding sea birds, including puffins and guillemots.

The coastline of this region is not very interesting, and it is one of the few parts of the Icelandic coast with no fishing ports. There are few settlements of any size at all. The only coastal town in the area is **Vík**, while the sole settlement between Mýrdalsjökull and Vatnajökull is the former religious site of **Kirkjubæjarklaustur**. In the western part of the region are the largely modern towns of **Hvolsvöllur** and **Hella**, located in the middle of an area that is rich in associations with the *Njáls Saga*.

THE VATNAJÖKULL AREA ★★★

The facts and figures applied to the Vatnajökull icecap are impressive in themselves. It is Europe's largest ice-sheet and the third largest in the world (after Antarctica and Greenland). It covers an area of 8538km² (3296 sq miles), which is approximately 8 per cent of Iceland. Its central plateau lies around 1500m (4900ft) above sea level, with fringing *nunataks* (mountain peaks protruding above the ice) such as **Barðarbunga**, at 2009m (6591ft), and **Hvannadalshnjúkur**, which at 2119m (6952ft) is

Iceland's highest mountain. It is estimated that the icecap is over 1000m (3280ft) thick in places. Whereas the Ice Age ended around 8000BC in most parts of Europe, the base of the ice on Vatnajökull dates from the start of the 1st century AD. Because of the high precipitation in the area and the fact that the accumulation of snow in winter is greater than the rate of melting in summer, the ice has built up rapidly. On the other hand, global warming has led to the retreat of the glacier snouts over the last two decades, leaving meltwater lakes between terminal moraines and the ice front. These features can easily be seen on **Kvíájökull**, **Fjallsjökull** and **Svínafellsjökull**, three glacial tongues just to the northwest of Höfn.

Owing to the dangerous conditions on Vatnajökull, excursions are best confined to organized tours. The usual route to the icecap is from the Ring Road up a track to the Skálafellsjökull mountain hut. Here, opportunity to sample glacier buggies and snowmobiles abounds. There are also cross-country ski options.

> **THE VATNAJÖKULL GLACIER BURST**
>
> In September 1996, the **Grímsvötn** subglacial volcano on Vatnajökull erupted, sending a column of steam over 10,000m (33,000ft) into the sky. The magma melted the ice, forming a huge subglacial lake. Just over a month later the waters of the lake rose and drained in a massive glacial burst, or *jökulhlaup*, causing an estimated 3000 billion cubic litres of water to pour down onto the coastal plain within a few hours. The protective dykes proved useless and some 1200m (3500ft) of Ring Road bridges were destroyed. Believed to have been Iceland's fourth largest volcanic eruption this century, it was seen on television screens throughout the world.

Jökulsárlón ***

Many visitors vote Jökulsárlón to be the highlight of their Icelandic experiences. It is an impressive glacial lagoon located at the snout of Breiðamerkurjökull glacier, which calves off icebergs into the lake. These icebergs are varied in colour – some white, some blue, others black or striped with volcanic ash. As they melt, they crack and crash around. The whole lagoon is incredibly beautiful and the icebergs can be viewed at close hand from an amphibious boat. Seals occasionally pop up their heads as the boat drifts

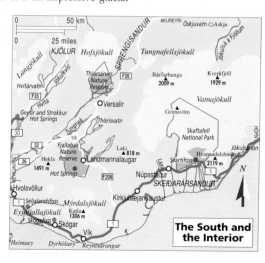

The South and the Interior

past. The lagoon was used for several scenes in the James Bond film *A View to a Kill*. All the service buses that travel along the Ring Road stop at the lake, where there are toilets, a restaurant and a campsite. It is well worth walking from the lagoon to the sea. The lagoon is drained by the **River Jökulsá** (almost certainly Iceland's shortest glacial river), which runs under the suspension bridge carrying the Ring Road before reaching the sea about 200m (220yd) or so away. Icebergs are quite frequently washed down the river and many of them become stranded on the beach, where they gradually melt away, forming curious shapes in the process.

Sandur Country **

A few kilometres west of Jökulsárlón, the first of the *sandurs* are encountered. These desert-like areas are plains of gravel and sand interspersed with a host of ever-changing braided streams. Much of the material is deposited during glacial bursts, or *jökulhlaups*. The largest of the *sandur* is **Skeiðarársandur**, which is fed from the Skeiðarárjökull glacier. The *sandurs* have always

Left: *Svartifoss (Black Falls), named after the dark columns of basalt that occur to either side of the falls.*
Opposite: *Melting icebergs assume these strange shapes in the Jökulsárlón glacial lake.*

presented problems for transport, and it was not until 1974 that the Ring Road was completed in this area. Even so, the road can be temporarily put out of use after a *jökulhlaup*, such as the one which occurred in 1996.

SKAFTAFELL NATIONAL PARK ★★★

Tucked into a sheltered south-facing lobe of the Vatnajökull icecap is Iceland's largest National Park, Skaftafell. In terms of visitor numbers it is one of the most popular locations in the country. Founded in 1967 (as a joint venture between the government and the World Wildlife Fund), the park covers 1600km^2 (617 sq miles). It includes such diverse landscapes as ice sheet, glaciers, tumbling glacial rivers, waterfalls, luxuriant vegetation and moorland. Add a variety of bird life and abundant wild flowers and Skaftafell's popularity is understandable. It also has the benefit of a superb microclimate, situated as it is in a sheltered sunny position.

Skaftafell has a number of good hiking trails, the most popular of which is to the **Skaftafellsjökull glacier**, the snout of which is black with rubble and volcanic material. This takes around two hours return, but there are many hikes of longer duration with marvellous views of the glacial features. Another attraction is the **Svartifoss** waterfall, named after the black basalt columns along the lip of the falls and the valley sides, which are said to be

Above: *Iceland's most popular campsite, in the Skaftafell National Park. On summer weekends it will be crowded.*

the inspiration for many public buildings around the country. Svartifoss is reached by the path from the campground. Allow 1½ hours for the return walk. It is also worth continuing along the track to the west of the falls to **Sjónarsker**, a prominent rock with a viewing disc, giving panoramas towards the *sandur* and the coast. Skaftafell is of great interest to wildlife enthusiasts. Over 200 species of plant have been recorded here, while trees include rowan, birch and willow, some of which are quite tall (in Icelandic terms). Many of the typical highland bird species are found here, including golden plovers, redwings, ptarmigan, snipe and meadow pipits, all of which breed in the park.

Park Practicalities

Skaftafell is very accessible, being so close to the Ring Road, and the BSÍ Reykjavík–Höfn buses also stop here. The park's facilities include a car park, campsite, service area with restaurant, coffee shop, supermarket and an information centre. Detailed maps of the park are available in the shop. Skaftafell's popularity, however, comes with a price. On summer weekends it can become extremely crowded, and the noisy campsite has been likened to a 'tented refugee site'.

WEST OF SKAFTAFELL

The Ring Road at this point crosses the northern side of Skeiðarársandur. After about 35km (22 miles), the little hamlet of **Núpsstaður** is reached. Backed by the steep cliffs of Lómagnúpur, which rise to 767m (2550ft), the

---

SAFETY ON THE ICECAPS

Nature rules on the Icelandic icecaps, and the country's history is full of examples of accidents and tragedies which have befallen foolhardy travellers. Heavy snow, strong winds and whiteouts can occur at any time, even in summer, and crevasses can be deep and treacherous. Experts suggest that no climbing should take place at all in winter. Visitors in summer should be well equipped, know the routes, check the prevailing conditions and be aware of how to contact the rescue services in case of an emergency. Better still, go on a professionally led tour.

settlement of Núpsstaður was once an ecclesiastical centre. All that remains today is a collection of working farm buildings plus a delightful turf-roofed church. Made of stone and wood, the church dates from 1756 and is probably the smallest place of worship in Iceland. It was restored in the 1930s, and services are still held annually on the first Sunday in August. The key can be obtained from the farmhouse.

Klaustur ***

The only settlement of any size between Vík and Höfn is the unpronounceable **Kirkjubæjarklaustur**, generally known as 'Klaustur'. The modern appearance of this village belies its fascinating history. It was first inhabited by Irish monks before they were driven away by the Vikings. Later, in 1186, a Benedictine convent was established here, but it was disbanded in the mid-16th century during the Reformation. This may not have been a bad thing, as two of the nuns are said to have been burnt at the stake – one for criticizing the Pope and the other for sleeping with the Devil! In 1783 Kirkjubæjarklaustur was threatened by lava from the Laki eruptions (a series of fissures to the north of the village). The local priest, Jon Steingrímsson, is reported to have assembled all the inhabitants in the church and delivered a 'fire and brimstone sermon'. When the service was over, the congregation went outside only to find that the lava had miraculously been diverted past the village. A modern **Steingrímsson Memorial Chapel** was built in 1974, on the site of the original church, to commemorate the priest's *eldmessa*, or 'fire sermon'. One strange feature which should not be missed is the **Kirkjugólf**, a more or less flat rock surface

> **AVIAN PIRATES**
>
> **Skuas** are large hawk-like sea birds with generally dark plumage and angled wings when in flight. Their behaviour is often described as 'piratical', as they will chase and harass other birds until they disgorge their food. **Arctic skuas** are common throughout Iceland and will chase, in particular, Arctic terns. The **Great skua** is the largest of the skua family and will attack sea birds as large as gannets. It is known to kill small gulls by drowning them. The great skua is especially common as a nesting bird on the *sandur* to the south of Vatnajökull. Skuas are migrant birds and spend the winter months along the more southerly shores of the North Atlantic.

Below: *Hexagonal blocks of basalt at Klaustur, once thought to be the floor of an old church.*

covering some 80m² (280ft²). This was always thought to be the floor of an old church, which was reasonable considering the ecclesiastical background of the area. It is now known, however, that this is an entirely natural feature – the smoothed upper surface of a series of basalt columns. Kirkjubæjarklaustur today has a small airstrip and acts as a service centre for the surrounding farming community, as well as making a good base from which to explore the area.

Vík í Mýrdal *

At the eastern end of the *sandur* is Vík, the southernmost town of mainland Iceland and also, reputedly, the rainiest. Once a fishing port, the town abandoned this activity during the 19th century as it lacked a harbour. It is now a service and transport centre. An attractive town of some 400 inhabitants, Vík has the Mýrdalsjökull as a backdrop, with the steep-sided, flat-topped headland of Reynisfjall to the west. To the east stretches a beach of black volcanic sand, pounded by huge North Atlantic waves. This was the only non-tropical beach to be listed by the US magazine *Islands* as one of the Top Ten in the world. However, this is definitely not a beach for sitting on, not only because of the weather, but because of the colony of aggressive Arctic terns who resent human interference at breeding time.

Below: *The small regional centre of Vík. Its black sand beach, pounded by the Atlantic waves, has a breeding colony of rather aggressive Arctic terns.*

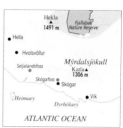

Left: *The distinctive sea stacks off the coast of Vík have breeding colonies of sea birds such as fulmars and guillemots.*

In Vík itself there are few sites to visit, except perhaps the delightful church occupying a dominating clifftop position. Boat trips, in an amphibious vehicle, run to the sea-bird cliffs in summer, but calm seas are essential for the cruises to operate.

Along the Coast ***

Just offshore from Vík are the photogenic black sea stacks of **Reynisdrangar**. Both the stacks and the headland are filled with breeding sea birds during the summer months, including razorbills, fulmars, guillemots and a large colony of puffins. On the far side of Reynisfjall is another headland called **Dyrhólaey**. It is 120m (390ft) high and incorporates a natural arch, through which small boats can pass during calm weather. Nearby is the large shallow lagoon of **Dyrhólaós**, another good bird-watching site. Away to the northwest is the hill of Pétursey, about 275m (900ft) high, which was an island before it became surrounded by glacial deposits.

MÝRDALSJÖKULL ***

Mýrdalsjökull is one of Iceland's major icecaps. It is the fourth largest in size, covering some 700km² (270 sq miles) and reaching 1480m (4855ft) in height. Like the larger Vatnajökull to the east, it receives high precipitation, up to 8000mm (315in) annually, so that the accumulation of ice has been significant, reaching a

---

THE REYNISDRANGAR 'NEEDLES'

Sea stacks are erosion features formed by wave action. The distinctive Reynisdrangar 'Needles' near Vík are some of Iceland's best examples of stacks. The highest of the stacks rises over 66m (216ft) above sea level. Legend has it that they were formed one night when two trolls were trying to drag a three-masted ship ashore. When daylight broke it was revealed that the ship had turned to stone.

Above: *View south from the Mýrdalsjökull icecap to the coastal lowlands.*

depth of over 1000m (3280ft). Like Vatnajökull, it also has a subglacial volcano, **Katla**, which has erupted 16 times since Iceland was settled. Each *jökulhlaup* has deposited great quantities of sand and gravel, so building up the **Mýrdalssandur**, which covers 70km² (270 sq miles). The Katla *jökulhlaups*, when in full flow, are estimated to contain a volume of water between five and seven times that of the Amazon River.

To the north of Mýrdalsjökull and immediately east of Hekla lies the **Landmannalaugar** area, famed for the variable colours in the rhyolite rocks.

The Skógar Area **

The small settlement of **Skógar**, nestling beneath the Mýrdalsjökull icecap, makes a good centre from which to explore the area. Just east of the village is the short glacial **Jökulsá River**, which is often called the Fúlilækur, or 'foul river'. The stench is caused by large quantities of sulphur which the river washes down from Katla. The main attraction in Skógar itself is the **Folk Museum**, which is located in a complex of turf farmhouses that have been reassembled on the site. The museum has over 6000 artefacts reflecting life in southern Iceland over the centuries. It is open from 09:00–18:00 during the summer months. Skógar's other attraction is one of Iceland's

highest waterfalls, **Skógafoss**, where, just west of the
village, the river Skóga drops 60m (196ft) into a narrow
gorge. Further west is another waterfall worth visiting.
This is **Seljalandsfoss**. It is possible to take the path
behind the falls, although a change in wind direction can
make this a drenching experience.

The West of the Region ***

There are two modern settlements located in the west of
southern Iceland. **Hella** has developed in recent years as
a market town, but has little to interest the tourist.
Hvolsvöllur, to the east, is another market town which
has a good view of snow-capped Hekla to the north. The
Hvolsvöllur area has numerous associations with the
Njáls Saga and guided tours to the main sites can be
arranged from the town.

THE INTERIOR

Although one of the most seductive parts of the country,
the interior of Iceland has a very limited access. It is only
open to traffic from late June to the end of August, and
even during this period four-wheel-drive vehicles are
essential. Even during the summer months, bad weather
can descend very rapidly and roads can become im-
passable. The interior is, nevertheless, a part of Iceland

FOLLOWING THE *NJÁLS SAGA*

The most popular and blood-
thirsty of the Sagas is certainly
the ***Njáls Saga***, the setting
for which was the land to the
north of **Hvolsvöllur**. The
story includes characters such
as Hallgeður Longlegs, Gissur
the White, and various
members of the Njál family.
The Saga features murder,
arson, betrayal, love, and a
continuous family feud –
indeed, an ancient version of
a modern-day soap opera!
Archaeological digs in the
20th century suggest that
much of the story may be
true. Visitors can go to the
Saga Centre in Hvolsvöllur,
and guided tours are available
to the sites mentioned in the
Njáls Saga. (tel: 487 8138).

Below: *A distant view
of the volcano Hekla. It
has erupted frequently
over historic time.*

which all visitors should experience if at all possible. It has been described as one of Europe's last wilderness areas, and travellers should be aware that there are few services available – no accommodation, no petrol stations, no restaurants and, in places, not even a road!

Kjölur Route

Most of the routes start in the southwest and end up in the north near Akureyri, Sauðarkrókur or Mývatn. The **Kjölur Route** runs northeast from the Gullfoss area and passes over the Central Highland desert, the track rising to over 700m (2300ft) between the Langjökull and Hofsjökull icecaps. It also passes the Hveravellir geothermal area, with its fumeroles and hot springs, before dropping down to meet the northern arm of the Ring Road near Blönduós. Although it is the easiest of the routes through the interior, it was unpopular for many centuries as it was often the haunt of bandits.

Sprengisandur Route

The alternative **Sprengisandur Route** initially follows the valley of the Thjórsá River before crossing the pass at around 800m (2625ft) between the Hofsjökull and the smaller Tungnafellsjökull icecaps. It then follows the Skjálfandafljót valley northwards to join the Ring Road near Goðafoss. This is a more difficult and hostile route, but gives some superb views of the icecaps.

Right: *A super jeep with enlarged wheels crosses a river in spate in central Iceland. The general advice to motorists is to travel in convoys and get accurate weather forecast before making a crossing.*

South Iceland at a Glance

June–September has the best weather, but rain can be expected all year, with deep snowfalls on the higher land. On weekends in July–August popular spots like Skaftafell can become uncomfortably crowded. The interior is rarely open for tourists before late June. Winter snows begin again by mid-September.

BSÍ buses on the Reykjavík–Höfn service use the southern arm of the Ring Road and stop at the main tourist 'honeypots'. There are no internal airports in the region, although there are a few private airstrips.

Service buses using the Ring Road are few and far between and visitors on a budget may find it more convenient to hitch lifts in summer when the roads are busy. A private car is most convenient. This is also true of travelling in the interior, where 4WD is essential.

There is nothing in the luxury classification in south Iceland, but plenty of mid-range choices although these fill up rapidly in the height of the season.

MID-RANGE
The **Edda Group** have summer hotels at Kirkjubæjarklaustur, Skógar and Holsvöllur. For booking, tel: 505 0910.

Hotel Holsvöllur, Hliðarvegur 7, 860 Holsvöllur, tel: 487 8050, fax: 487 8058, e-mail: hotelvolsvollur@simnet.is
Hotel Ásgarður, v/Hvolsvöll, 860 Hólsvöllur, tel: 487 8367, fax: 487 8387, e-mail: asgard@isholf.is
Viking theme hotel on edge of town. Some cottages available.
Hotel Vík í Mýrdal, v/Klettsvegur, 870 Vík, tel: 487 1480, fax: 487 1302, e-mail: hotelvik@ka.is
Between cliff and beach.

BUDGET
Gistiheimilið Húsið, Fljóshlíð, 861 Hvolsvöllur, tel: 487 8448, fax: 487 8748. Small guest-house on outskirts of town. Horse riding can be arranged.
Farmhouse accommoda-tion; for details and booking, tel: 562 3640.
There are **Youth Hostels** at **Fljötsdalur**, near Holsvöllur, at **Reynisbrekka**, outside Vík, and at **Vagnsstaðir**, west of Höfn. Booking, tel: 553 8110.
Official campsites in the area have excellent facilities. The more popular ones, such as in the Skaftafell National Park, can become very crowded on weekends in the summer.

Good restaurants are rather hard to find. The best bets are dining rooms of larger hotels, though they may be expensive. Snack bars at petrol stations are good value and offer a wholesome tourist menu.

Most excursions here involve the icecaps of Vatnajökull and Mýrdalsjökull. Many of these can be booked in Reykjavík with firms such as Reykjavík Excursions or BSÍ. Local firms run snowmobile and glacier buggy tours on the icecaps. For trips on Mýrdalsjökull, con-tact **Geysir Snjósleðaferðir**, tel: 568 8888. For trips on Vatnajökull, contact **Glacier Tours**, tel: 478 1000. For boat trips on Jökulsá Lagoon, **Won-der Boat Trips**, tel: 478 1065.

There are several **Tourist Information Centres** in the area. The largest centre is in the **Skaftafell National Park**, tel: 478 1627. Others are at **Skógar**, tel: 487 8843; **Kirkjubæjarklaustur**, tel: 4874620; **Vík**, tel: 487 1395; **Holsvöllur**, tel: 487 8781; and **Hella**, tel: 487 5165.

VÍK	J	F	M	A	M	J	J	A	S	O	N	D
AVE. TEMP. °C	-0.4	0.2	0.7	3.2	6.5	9.4	11.2	10.4	7.5	4.5	1.1	-0.4
AVE. TEMP. °F	31.3	32.4	33.3	37.8	43.7	48.9	52.2	50.7	45.5	40.1	34	31.3
AVE. RAINFALL mm	145	130	130	115	118	131	121	159	141	185	137	133
AVE. RAINFALL in	5.71	5.12	5.12	4.53	4.65	5.16	4.77	6.26	5.55	7.29	5.39	5.24

8
The Westman Islands

The *Vestmannaeyjar*, or Westman Islands, are a group of 15 islands and rock skerries some 11km (7 miles) off the southern coast of Iceland. Only one, the largest, known as **Heimaey** (pronounced *hay may*), is inhabited. The islands are located on the Mid-Atlantic Ridge and are of recent geological origin. They were formed of volcanic material, spewed out of submarine volcanoes between 8000 and 3000BC. This process has continued into the 20th century with the formation of the new island of **Surtsey**, created by an eruption which lasted for four years, between 1963 and 1967. The eruption was seen on television screens around the world, and scientific studies of the volcano have continued to this day. Ten years later, an eruption occurred on Heimaey, which forced the evacuation of the entire population, fortunately without loss of life. After this new volcano, named **Eldfell**, had quietened down, the inhabitants returned to find that the island had grown in size by 15 per cent and that the lava flow had improved the shelter around the harbour.

A Violent History

The history of the Westman Islands has been typified by violence and tragedy. The islands were first inhabited by a group of **Irish slaves** (these 'Westmen' may have given the islands their name) intent on escape after murdering their master, Hjörleifur Hróðmarsson, the foster brother of Ingólfur Arnarson, in turn recognized as the first genuine Icelandic settler. When Ingólfur heard the news, he quickly tracked down the slaves and killed

DON'T MISS

** **Thjódhátíð:** the Westman Islands' National Day held on the first weekend in August.
* **Heimaey's volcanoes:** easy hiking trails over both the old and new volcanoes of Helgafell and Eldfell.
* **The Aquarium:** at Heimaey's Natural History Museum, with several rare North Atlantic fish.
* **Sea-bird cliffs:** on the north of Heimaey and also on other islands, with thousands of puffins.

Opposite: *The sea cliffs of Heimaey, famous for their nesting puffins.*

CLIMATE

The Westman Islands' maritime position has the effect of moderating the climate, making it milder than that of Reykjavík in winter, but cooler in summer. **Rainfall** is high, with an annual total of 1713mm (67.5 in). Average temperatures in **January** stay above freezing, and any snowfall is light. The average **July** temperature is 9.6°C (49°F), which is lower than that of the mainland. Fog and low cloud are common.

Below: *The town of Heimaey has frequently been threatened by volcanic activity. The last lava flow in 1973 destroyed some of the houses but actually improved the harbour.*

them. The very first permanent settler in the Westman Islands, probably around 900, is believed to have been **Herjólfur Barðursson**, who was looking for a peaceful escape from the feuding on the mainland. The first church was built around 1000, and shortly afterwards the islands were purchased by the **Bishops of Skálholt**. Later British traders took over the islands as their headquarters in the North Atlantic until they were driven out by the Danes in the mid-16th century.

In 1627 the Westman Islands were attacked by a group of **North African pirates**, who murdered over 40 people and took away around 250 hostages, most of whom were sold as slaves in the markets of Morocco. By this time the Bishops of Skálholt had turned the islands over to the King of Norway. The succeeding centuries saw further tragedies – disease, starvation, scurvy and dysentry. The **Laki eruptions** in 1783 and the subsequent 'haze fires' killed most of the livestock and poisoned the sea. The 20th century saw a change in fortunes, with the development of the fishing industry, but a further setback came in 1973 with the **eruption of Eldfell**. After the evacuation of Heimaey, many of the inhabitants, who returned to find their houses destroyed by lava, decided to emigrate to other countries.

Today, the Westman Islands are thriving. Prosperity is based almost entirely on the **fishing** industry and the majority of the 5300 residents are involved in fishing or tourism. The first freezing plant was installed in 1908 and shortly afterwards the islands were connected with the mainland by submarine electricity and telephone cables and a freshwater pipeline. The Westman Islands have a fishing fleet of over 100 vessels, which account for around 15 per cent of Iceland's total exports. The main fish caught are sole, cod, halibut and haddock. There are also salmon farms which are located in the outer harbour. Some of the fish is exported fresh, but the majority is processed on Heimaey.

Left: *View of Heimaey harbour. The port accounts for 15 per cent of Iceland's fish exporting business.*

HEIMAEY **

The only inhabited island in *Vestmannaeyjar* is **Heimaey** (the 'home island'). The other islands are too steep-sided for harbours, although some are used for summer sheep pastures. The town of Heimaey is attractively located around the **harbour** and stretches southward to cover about a third of the island. To the north of the town are some sheer cliffs, while to the south the lava flow from the 1973 eruption has contrived to make a sheltered entrance to the harbour. Look out for the **mural** on the side of one of the buildings near the harbour. It was painted by local schoolchildren and depicts the town on the morning of the 1973 eruption. Forming the southeastern background to the town are the two low volcanic peaks of **Helgafell** and the more recent **Eldfell**.

THJÓÐHÁTÍÐ

The main social event of the Westman Islands' calendar is their annual **National Day** held over the first weekend in August. It began in 1874, when bad weather prevented the islanders from reaching the mainland to celebrate Iceland's National Day. They therefore decided to hold their own festival a month later, and this has now become an annual tradition. The festivities take place in a large valley called **Herjólfsdalur**, which becomes a huge campsite for the occasion. It is the location for singing, dancing, much drinking and a large bonfire. Some mainland critics disapprove, suggesting that the festival has become a mere showpiece for supporters of Vestmannæyjar independence. Nevertheless, it is hugely enjoyed by both islanders and those who come over from the mainland to join in the celebrations.

Above: *An aerial view of Heimaey town and harbour.*
Opposite: *Eldfell rises to 205m (672ft) and can be climbed from Heimaey town.*

Visitors arrive at Heimaey by air or ferry, and there is enough to see here to make a two- or three-day stay worthwhile. Despite the existence of coaches and taxis, most of the island can be covered **on foot**.

Museums ***

Heimaey's **Natural History Museum**, at Heiðarvegur 12, tel: 481 1997, was established in 1964. It has the usual selection of geological specimens and stuffed birds, but the highlight is the aquarium, which has a wonderful collection of Icelandic fish, both common and rare. Open from 11:00–17:00, May to September.

The **Folk Museum** is located above the library, tel: 481 1194. This museum combines an art gallery with a collection of stamps, currency and historic household artefacts. Open 14:00–17:00 daily during the summer.

The **Volcano Show** is a film show which takes place in the Félagsheimilið theatre / community centre, with performances during the summer at 15:00, 17:00 and 21:00, each lasting 55 minutes. Two films are shown: one

---

SURTSEY

In November 1963 a new volcano rose from the sea bed about 18km (11 miles) southwest of Heimaey. This was named **Surtsey** after the legendary Norse giant **Surtur**. The eruptions lasted for four years, and at their peak sent up a column of steam and ash over 10,000m (33,000ft) into the sky. When the activity calmed down, Surtsey had reached a height of 150m (492ft) and covered an area of 3km² (11 sq miles). Thereafter Surtsey became a natural laboratory for scientists, who have observed its gradual colonization by insects, birds, plants, and mammals such as seals. Surtsey is still off-limits to visitors, but it is possible to fly over the dormant volcano in a chartered light aircraft.

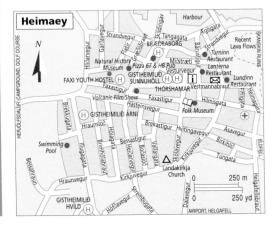

records the 1973 eruptions and the rescue operations, and the other tells the story of a fisherman whose boat capsized 5km (3 miles) offshore. He spent six hours in the icy waters before coming ashore over sharp lava rocks and reaching safety. A London medical expert later concluded that the fisherman had the body fat of a seal!

Other points of interest ***

Heimaey's modern white **church** is worth a look. Opposite the entrance is a memorial to lost fishermen. An older stone church, the **Landakirkja**, dates from 1788. It has an unusual interior arrangement, in that the pulpit is placed immediately behind the altar. The Landakirkja is open daily from 13:00–14:00 in July and August. The most recent **lava flows** are readily accessible and give good views over the harbour and also towards the mainland, where the Vatnajökull and Mýrdalsjökull icecaps can be seen on a clear day. **Eldfell**, which rises to 205m (672ft), can quite easily be climbed on the pathways, some with artificial steps, leading up to the crater rim. There are still plenty of hot cinders and fumeroles, so stout footwear is recommended. Be prepared, too, for the stench of sulphur. The slightly higher **Helgafell** can also be climbed. This was formed about 5000 years ago and rises to a height of 226m (741ft). Take the path from the end of the football pitch.

HEIMAEY'S LATEST VOLCANIC EPISODE

In January 1973 a serious volcanic eruption occurred on the eastern side of the island of Heimaey. Fortunately, the fishing fleet was in the harbour and able to evacuate the entire population of 5300 people. A massive amount of lava and ash threatened the town, demolishing houses and causing fires. The greatest danger was that the lava flow, which was 165m (540ft) high, would block the harbour entrance. Without the harbour, the evacuation of Heimaey would have been permanent. The flow was eventually stopped by spraying it with millions of gallons of sea water. The island had increased in size by 15 per cent and over half the town had been destroyed. The good news was that the lava flow now actually protected the harbour entrance, while the high underground temperatures could be used to provide the island with hot water and heating.

PUFFINS

The puffin (*Fratercula arctica*), with its upright stance and parrot-like beak on a disproportionately large head, is everyone's favourite sea bird. Both the birds and their eggs have always been eaten in Iceland, and puffin meat is still a traditional dish on the Westman Islands' National Day. The birds are caught in nets on the end of long poles, and in the past a good puffin-catcher has been known to capture over 1000 birds in a single day. Today, few puffins are caught. Baby puffins are usually deserted by their parents and left to find their own way to the sea. Many become disorientated by the lights of Heimaey and can be seen wandering around the town. At this time they are collected up by the children of Heimaey and released into the sea.

Boat trips from Heimaey ***

There are a number of boat trips from Heimaey. The tours usually pass the salmon farms, the pen where Keiko the killer whale resided for a number of years (*see* panel, page 12), and the sea-bird cliffs. On calm days the boats go right in amongst the caves and stacks along the coast. Sea-fishing and whale-watching trips are also available.

Sport ***

The Westman Islands have what is arguably Iceland's best 18-hole **golf course**, located in Herjólfsdalur. It is the country's most southerly golf course, and the mild climate that generally prevails in this part of the country means that it is playable for much of the year. There is also a superb **indoor swimming pool**, complete with sauna, jacuzzi, solarium and gym.

Bird-watching on the Westman Islands

The Westman Islands form one of the prime sea-bird haunts in Northern Europe. Several spectacular cliffs (particularly on northern Heimaey) and rich food in the sea have led to quite amazing numbers of nesting sea birds. The islands support Iceland's only breeding colonies of manx shearwater, Leach's petrel and storm petrel. However, as these birds are largely nocturnal in their habits, observation is difficult. There are vast numbers of **gannets**, particularly on the smaller outer islands. Other species include five types of auk, fulmars and gulls. By far the most common sea bird, however, is the **puffin**, with literally hundreds of thousands of nesting pairs. Though the puffin was once part of the staple diet of the Westman Islanders, human predation never seemed to affect the numbers of this endearing bird.

Below: *Too cute to eat? Puffin is still a delicacy in the Westman Islands.*

The Westman Islands at a Glance

BEST TIMES TO VISIT

Snowfall is low in winter, but rain and mist occur year-round. July and August are warmest. National Day (in August) is a good time to visit.

GETTING THERE

A **car ferry** from Thorlákshöfn (with bus connection to Reykjavík) to Heimaey runs daily, with extra crossings in summer and at weekends. The trip takes two hours on rough seas. Tel: 481 2800, 481 3915 or 552 2300. Íslandsflug and Flugleiðir run daily **flights** from Reykjavík Domestic Airport. It takes 30 minutes in good weather, but cancellations do occur due to fog. Information, tel: 481 3300.

GETTING AROUND

Most of Heimaey can easily be seen on foot as it covers only 13.4km^2 (5.2 sq miles). For local **taxis**, tel: 481 2038. **Car hire** is also available, but very expensive, tel: 481 2038.

WHERE TO STAY

MID-RANGE
Hotel Thórshamar, Vestmannabraut 28, tel: 481 2900, fax: 481 1696, e-mail: thorshamar @eyjar.is Heimaey's best hotel. Can arrange horse riding, sea fishing and bike hire.
Hotel Bræðraborg, Herjólfsgata 4, tel: 481 1515, fax: 481 2007. The Gistiheimilið Heimir in the same building offers a cheaper alternative. Has small tourist information office.

BUDGET
Gistiheimilið Árný, Illugagata 7, 900 Vestmannaeyjar, tel and fax: 481 2082. Near pool. Cooking facilities available.
Gistiheimilið Hvíld, Höfðavegi 16, 900 Vestmannaeyjar, tel: 481 1230. Good value.
Gistiheimilið Sunnuhóll, Vestmannabraut 28, 900 Vestmannaeyjar, tel: 481 2900, fax: 481 1696. Comfortable guesthouse near the harbour.
Gistiheimilið Hreiðrið, Faxastígur 33, 900 Vestmannaeyjar, tel: 481 1045, fax: 4811414, e-mail eyjamyndir@ishilf.is Good wheelchair access. Probably the best budget option.
Faxi Youth Hostel, Faxastígur 38, 900 Vestmannaeyjar, tel: 481 2915, fax: 481 1497. Open Jun–Sep. Book in advance. The **Heimaey campsite** at Herjólfsdalur, tel: 481 2922, has good facilities.

WHERE TO EAT

Heimaey has a wide variety of eating places to suit all pockets. Hotel restaurants are generally the best, though also the most expensive. The **Hertoginn** in the Hotel Thórshamar is particularly recommended.
Lundinn, Kirkuvegur 21, tel: 481 1426. Has a good range of Westman Island specialities, including puffin and fish dishes. Live music on certain days.
Lanterna, Bárustígur 11, tel: 481 3393. Yugoslav-run. Good local food and Balkan dishes. For cheap pizzas, try **Pizza 67**, Heiðarvegur 5, tel: 481 1567, and **HB Pub**, tel: 481 1515, which has live music.

TOURS AND EXCURSIONS

Páll Helgason Travel Service (PH Tours) run daily **coach tours** of Heimaey. Booking is through Hotel Bræðraborg. PH Tours also organizes **boat trips** around the coastline, visiting stacks, sea caves and bird cliffs. Other boat trips are run by Hjálmar Guðnasson, tel: 481 1195, and Ólafur Tyr Guðjónsson, tel: 481 2333. Margo Renner, tel: 481 2269, organizes **hiking trips** to bird cliffs and volcanic locations.

USEFUL CONTACTS

The **Tourist Information Centre** is at Vestmannabraut 38, tel: 481 1271, fax: 481 2792. Open 09:00–12:00 and 13:00–16:00, Mon–Fri, and 13:00–16:00 at weekends. There is also a small tourist information office at the Hotel Bræðraborg, tel: 481 2922.

HEIMAEY	J	F	M	A	M	J	J	A	S	O	N	D
AVE. TEMP. °C	1.3	2.0	1.7	3.4	5.6	8.0	9.8	9.6	7.4	5.0	2.4	1.4
AVE. TEMP. °F	34.3	35.6	35.1	38.1	42.1	46.4	49.6	49.3	45.3	41.0	36.3	34.5
AVE. RAINFALL mm	158	139	141	117	105	102	95	140	131	162	154	143
AVE. RAINFALL in	6.23	5.48	5.55	4.61	4.14	4.02	3.74	5.52	5.16	6.38	6.07	5.63

Travel Tips

Tourist Information

The **Icelandic Tourist Board** has offices in Copenhagen (Denmark), Paris (France), Neu Isenberg and Frankfurt (Germany), Tokyo (Japan), Zürich (Switzerland), London (United Kingdom) and New York (USA). For information in UK contact Icelandair Holidays, 172 Tottenham Court Road London WIP OLY, tel: 020 7874 1000, website: www. icetourist.is. The main office in Iceland is the **Tourist Information Centre**, Bankastræti 2, Reykjavík, tel: 562 3045, fax: 562 4749. Information is also available at Reykjavík's City Hall in Vonarstræti. Regional offices in Akranes, Akureyri, Egilsstaðir, Húsavík, Ísafjörður, and Sauðárkrókur provide brochures and pamphlets, have information about tour operators and assist in booking accommodation and flights.

Entry Requirements

A valid passport is required for all visitors, except those from Nordic countries, who only need an identity card. Visas are needed for visitors from certain countries, which do not include Canada, USA, the EU, Australia and many others. If in doubt, ask at an Icelandic embassy or consulate before departure. An entry stamp in a passport is valid for 3 months.

Customs

Visitors over the age of 20 may bring in free of duty one litre of spirits or wine and 200 cigarettes. The duty-free shop at Keflavík Airport is open to arriving passengers and in view of the high cost of living in Iceland it is advisable to make use of this. There are restrictions on most meat and dairy products, but visitors may bring in up to 10kg of other foods. Icelandic VAT is high, but much of this can be refunded on leaving if goods are bought at special tax-free shops.

Health Requirements

Iceland has no specific health problems and inoculations are unnecessary. All health services are publicly provided and free for citizens of Nordic and EU countries (bring form E1 11). Dental services are privately provided and costs are on par with Europe and the USA.

Getting There

By Air: The main airline serving Iceland is the national carrier **Icelandair** (tel: 569 0710), with services from Amsterdam, Baltimore, Barcelona, Bergen, Boston, Chicago, Copenhagen, Detroit, Faroe Islands, Frankfurt, Glasgow, Gothenburg, London, Luxembourg, Milan, New York, Orlando, Oslo, Paris, Salzburg, Stockholm and Washington DC. Icelandair offers passengers travelling between Europe and USA a stopover deal for up to 72 hours. **SAS** flies from Copenhagen, Oslo and Stockholm, while the budget airline **Iceland Express** flies to Keflavik from London and Copenhagen. All incoming international flights land at **Keflavík** Airport, 50km (31 miles) from Reykjavík. Regular non-stop coaches run from the airport to the capital, taking 45 minutes. The city terminal is at the Hotel Loftleiðir.

By Sea: The Faroes shipping company **Smyril Line** (tel: 562 6362) runs a car ferry service to Iceland from late May to early September. The weekly trip links Iceland with the Shetland and Faroe

Islands, Bergen (Norway) and Esbjerg (Denmark). The *MS Norröna* accommodates some 1000 passengers and 250 cars. The ferry arrives in Seyðis-fjörður, which is over 700km (435 miles) from Reykjavík along the northern or south-ern routes of the Ring Road.

What to Pack

The unpredictable weather means that visitors should be prepared for anything. Wind and rain can be incessant, so water- and windproof jacket and trousers are essential. Sweater, scarf, hat and gloves are also advisable. A pair of hik-ing boots are necessary, even on a coach tour, as most of the sites involve a walk, often over rough ground. Bring a swimsuit for the geothermally-heated swimming pools. Formal clothes are necessary in quality hotels and restaurants. The light provides marvellous con-ditions for photography. Most people underestimate the quantity of film they need and it is very expensive to buy, so bring supplies. Binoculars are essential for observing wildlife.

Money Matters

Icelandic currency is the **króna** (Ikr), divided into 100 aurar. Notes come in denominations of 5000 Ikr, 2000 Ikr, 1000 Ikr and 500 Ikr, and coins in 100 Ikr, 50 Ikr, 10 Ikr, 5 Ikr and Ikr. Currency may be bought abroad (sometimes with diffi-culty), but the local exchange rate is better. Three **banks** in Iceland – Búnðarbanki Íslands, Íslandsbanki and Landsbanki Íslands – usually open 09:15–

16:00, Mon–Fri; opening hours may be erratic in rural areas. There are exchange facilities at Keflavík Airport from 06:30–18:30. **Travellers cheques** may be cashed at most hotels. **ATM**s are common in Reyjavík and other towns and are increasingly found in rural areas. **Credit cards** can be used to obtain cash from banks and are widely accepted in hotels, shops and restaurants, but not always at petrol service stations. **VAT** on most pur-chases is currently at 24.5%.

Accommodation

Prices are high, particularly in **hotels**. Only Reykjavík and Akureyri have international-standard hotels offering *en-suite* bathrooms, restaurants, shops and often indoor pools. Tourist-class hotels throughout the country offer fewer facilit-ies, but most have a restaurant and rooms with a private shower and toilet. A unique Icelandic feature is the **sum-mer hotel**. These open for June and August but for the rest of the year they are board-ing schools and colleges. Facilities vary: some offer only **sleeping-bag accommoda-tion**, while others also have restaurants and pools. Most common budget accom-modation is the **guesthouse**. Located throughout the coun-try, they usually offer bed and breakfast. A list of hotels and guesthouses can be obtained from tourist information centres. Advance booking is advisable during peak season. **Farmhouse accommodation** is widely offered by Icelandic

farmers, usually on a bed and breakfast or sleeping bag arrangement. Some farms provide self-catering cottages, others have horses and boats for rent. A list of farms offering accommodation is found in the booklet *Icelandic Farm Holidays* from information centres.

Youth hostels are econom-ical and there are around 30 in the country. Most close in the winter. They usually offer sleeping-bag accommodation and cooking facilities, though some provide family rooms and meals. Pre-booking is essential in July and August. Contact the Icelandic Youth Hostels Association, tel: 553 8110, fax: 567 9201.

Despite the weather, **camping** is very popular. There are over 100 sites, often in national parks or scenic areas. Facilities vary – some are quite primitive, others have toilets, showers, snack bars, kitchens and pools. Note that facilities may not be

---

PUBLIC HOLIDAYS

New Year's Day • 1 January
Easter • Maundy Thursday, Good Friday, Easter Sunday, Easter Monday
First Day of Summer • Third Tuesday in April
Labour Day • 1 May
Ascension Day • May/June
Seamen's Day • Early June
Independence Day • 17 June
August Public Holiday • First Weekend in August
Rettir • September (sheep and horse round-ups in rural areas)
Christmas Eve • 24 December
Christmas Day • 25 December
Boxing Day • 26 December
New Year's Eve • 31 December

on the site but in the nearest settlement. When camping in non-designated areas, obtain the landowner's permission. Because of possible wind and rain, tents should be durable. The booklet *Camping in Iceland*, obtainable from all tourist information centres, has a list of officially designated sites. Hikers in remote areas can make use of **mountain huts**, which usually have only basic facilities. They are owned by the Touring Club of Iceland, tel: 568 2533, who charge a small fee for their use. Accommodation is limited to 3 nights; pre-booking is essential.

Eating Out

Food is a major expense. With a service charge, plus alcohol, the bill may be double that which tourists would pay at home. There are plenty of **restaurants** in Reykjavík and to a lesser extent in Akureyri,

but elsewhere they are mainly confined to hotels. Reykjavík has a range of ethnic restaurants, including Japanese, Indian, Thai, Italian and Chinese. Cheaper are the American fast-food chains, pizza restaurants and hot dogs stalls. In rural areas, cafés attached to service stations offer cheap, filling food, usually with a daily 'special'. In summer, look for the sign 'Tourist Menu' : this is usually soup, a main course and coffee for a set price. **Alcohol** is very expensive and can only be bought from State Monopoly Shops which have limited opening hours by those over 20. The traditional Icelandic tipple is *brennivin*, a schnapps made from potatoes and flavoured with caraway. The main brand is Svarti Dauði, which means 'Black Death'!

Transport

Iceland has no railways, so travel is mainly by road and air. **Air:** Difficult surface conditions, particularly in winter, mean that flights are a common way to get around. Most routes are operated by Icelandair's subsidiary Flugleðir. Other carriers are Norðurlands (at Akureyri) and Austurlands (at Egilsstaðir airport). Various bargain air passes are available, including Holiday Air Rover, offering round routing from Reykjavík via Akureyri, Egilsstaðir, Höfn, Ísafjörður and back to Reykjavík. The main centre for domestic flights is the Reykjavík Domestic Airport. **Road:** Iceland has a good network of roads, including Road

No.1, the so-called Ring Road, completed in 1974. About 80 per cent of the Ring Road is metalled, the rest gravel. During dry periods, the gravel roads can be dusty, and flying stones can damage cars. Tracks through the interior are usually open only in July–August and involve fording rivers, so 4WD vehicles are essential. Petrol is expensive, though diesel is relatively cheap. Driving is on the right and seat belts are obligatory. Headlights must remain on. Speed limits are 50 km/h (30 mph) in urban areas, 80 km/h (50 mph) outside towns. Look out for sheep in rural areas. Drunk driving regulations are strictly enforced and the legal limit is low. Drivers bringing their own cars to Iceland need a driving licence, registration document and green card. The Icelandic motoring organization (FÍB) will be allied to home organizations.
Car Hire: Most international car-hire companies, like Avis, Hertz and Budget, are based in Reykjavík. Car hire is expensive, mainly due to the 24 per cent VAT. If you plan to go off the metalled roads, a 4WD vehicle is recommended. Minimum age for car hire is 21 for saloon cars and 25 for an off-road vehicle. There is a high demand for car hire in summer and pre-booking is recommended.
Buses: A network of long-distance bus routes covering all the inhabited areas is co-ordinated BSÍ, based at the main bus terminal in Reykjavík (tel: 552 2300, fax:552 9973). Discount passes like the Full

GOOD READING

Peterson, Mountford and Hollom (1993) *Birds of Britain and Europe* (Collins).
Love, Askell (1983) *The Flora of Iceland* (Almenna Bokafelagid).
Wolesey, Pat (1979) *A Field Key to the Flowering Plants of Iceland* (The Thule Press).
Carwardine, Mark (1986) *Iceland: Nature's Meeting Place* (Iceland Review).
Perkins, John (1983) *Iceland: A Geological Field Guidebook* (Cardiff University).
Magnusson, Magnus (1990) *Iceland Saga* (The Bodley Head).
Sale, Richard (2000) *The Xenophobe's Guide to Icelanders* (Oval Books).

Circle Pass allow a complete circuit of the Ring Road in either direction with as many stops as required. Included in the price are 10 per cent discounts on accommodation and ferries. The Omnibus Pass allows unlimited travel on any bus route for a week and discounts on accommodation.

Taxis: Available in the main settlements, taxis are usually driver-owned but the fares are uniform and you pay what is on the meter. Fares are comparable to those in the USA and most European countries. You can also hire taxis for a flat rate to visit places of interest.

Ferries: Iceland has three car ferries – Reykjavík to Akranes, Thorlákshöfn to Heimaey, and a ferry linking Stykkishólmur, Flatey and Brjáslækur. There are also several passenger ferries.

Maps: The Globetrotter Travel Map of Iceland is excellent. For general purposes, free maps are available in tourist information centres and hotels. The Ferdakort map (1:500,000), as well as nine sectional 1:250,000 maps, are good, but expensive if the full set is bought. There is also an informative 1:500,000 geological map. All these maps are available at Landmælingar Íslands shop, Laugavegur 178, PO Box 5060, 125 Reykjavík.

Business Hours

Offices usually open 09:00–17:00, Monday–Friday. Shops stay open later, but may close on Saturdays in summer. Most supermarkets are open daily, also weekends and holidays. Banks open 09:15–16:00, Monday–Friday. Petrol stations open daily, 07:00–22:00.

Tipping

Service is included in prices for hotels, restaurants and taxis. Tipping is not customary.

Time Difference

Iceland is on Greenwich Mean Time (GMT) throughout the year. In summer it is one hour behind British Summer Time.

Communications

All Icelandic towns have post offices and telephone offices – look for the sign *Póstur og Sími* – usually open Monday–Friday, 08:30–17:00. Stamps are available in supermarkets

---

ROAD SIGNS

Iceland's roads are generally well signposted and distances clearly marked in kilometres. Road signs are the same as those used throughout the EU. The danger signal (an exclamation mark!) should always be heeded. Even the Ring Road has gravel stretches, so slow down when the 'loose stones' sign appears. When a tarmac surface ends it is marked by the sign *Malbik Endar*. Icelandic roads, including the Ring Road, have many single-lane bridges marked by *Einbreid Brú*. Blind summits, shown by *Blindhæd*, should be approached with caution – never stop on the top or sides of a blind summit.

---

and hotels. Post boxes are red and often found near hotels. Allow 3–5 days for a letter to reach Europe or North America. The telephone system is very efficient. Due to the climate, telephone booths are usually in hotels, restaurants and service stations. Subscribers in the telephone directory are listed by their first names. Digital dialling was introduced in 1995. There are no regional codes; the international code for Iceland is 354. If making international calls from Iceland, dial 00 first then the international code for the country concerned. For the UK this is 44, for Canada and USA it is 1. Many Icelanders have mobile phones. Visitors should have no difficulty in getting their mobile phones to work in Iceland, but reception is poor in the more mountainous and remote parts of the country.

CONVERSION CHART		
FROM	**TO**	**MULTIPLY BY**
Millimetres	Inches	0.0394
Metres	Yards	1.0936
Metres	Feet	3.281
Kilometres	Miles	0.6214
Square kilometres	Square miles	0.386
Hectares	Acres	2.471
Litres	Pints	1.760
Kilograms	Pounds	2.205
Tonnes	Tons	0.984
To convert Celsius to Fahrenheit: x 9 ÷ 5 + 32		

Internet
Icelanders have enthusiastically adopted information technology. It is estimated that there are 145,000 internet users.

Websites
www.destination-iceland.com Excellent for hiking information.
www.south.is
Travel in south Iceland.
www.travelnet.is
History, geography, culture, accommodations, restaurants, and travel options.
www.iceland.is
Official government website.
www.icetourist.is
The Iceland Tourist Board's outstanding website.

Electricity
Voltage is 220, 50 HZ AC, with two round pin prongs. Visitors may need adapters.

Weights and Measures
Iceland uses the metric system.

Health Precautions
Tap water often smells sulphurous, but is potable all over the country. Food is prepared under stringent health regulations, so health hazards are few. Visitors in winter should guard against hypothermia, while those travelling over snow and ice during summer should use a block to prevent sun and wind burn.

Health Services
The public health service is excellent. There are over 40 hospitals providing 3600 beds. Staff are well-trained and are familiar with English. Visitors

should have travel insurance to cover unexpected health problems, particularly if planning risky outdoor activities.

Personal Safety
Iceland has one of the lowest crime rates in the world. If it does occur it is usually petty and alcohol-related. Visitors will seldom feel threatened, but should take the usual precautions with money, passports and valuables. The **emergency** telephone number for police and other services is **112**.

Etiquette
Icelanders are very friendly people who do their best to make visitors welcome. They are proud of their country and its lack of pollution. Litter is almost nonexistent so please respect this tradition.

Language
Icelandic is a Germanic language and most closely associated with Faroese and Norwegian. It has changed little, so that Icelanders are still able to read the **Sagas** which were written 800 years ago. The alphabet has 34 letters, including a number of extra vowels and consonants. The grammar is extremely complicated. Icelanders try to protect their language from outside influence and develop their own words rather than use English words such as 'computer'. Fortunately for visitors, Icelanders are excellent linguists. Danish and English are compulsory in schools and many students also speak other languages.

USEFUL WORDS AND PHRASES

Yes, No • *Já, Nei*
Hello • *Góðen dag*
Goodbye • *Bless*
Thank you • *Takk fyrir*
How are you? • *Hvad sergirdu gott?*
Toilet • *Snyrting*
Ladies, Gents • *Konur, Karlar*
How much is it? • *Hvad kostar petta?*
Airport • *Flúgvöllur*
Ferry • *Ferja*
May I have • *Ma eg fá*
My name is • *Ég heiti*
Where are you from? • *Hva ðan ert pú?*
Cheers! • *Skál!*
I don't understand • *Ég skil ekki*
Guesthouse • *Gistheimili*
Youth hostel • *Farfuglaheimili*
Open • *Opið*
Closed • *Lokað*
Forbidden • *Bönnuð*
Beer • *Bjór*
Bread • *Brauð*
Coffee • *Kaffi*
Fish • *Fiskur*
Lamb • *Lambakjót*
Milk • *Mjólk*
Soup • *Súpa*
Tea • *Te*
Water • *Vatn*
Days of the week:
Sunnudagur, Mánudagur, Pri ðjudagur, Miðvikudagur, Fimmtudagur, Fostudagur, Laugardagur
Some numbers:
0 • *null*
1 • *einn*
2 • *tveir*
3 • *prir*
4 • *fjórir*
5 • *fimm*
6 • *sex*
7 • *sjö*
8 • *átta*
9 • *níu*
10 • *tíu*
100 • *hundrad*
1000 • *thúsund*
1,000,000 • *milljón*

INDEX

Note: Numbers in **bold** indicate photographs